How To Make a Great Presentation

In 2 Hours

The fastest, Easiest Way to Make a Presentation on the Market Today!

How To Make a Great Presentation

In 2 Hours

Frank Paolo

By One of Corporate America's Top Speaking Coaches

LIFETIME BOOKS
HOLLYWOOD

This publication is designed to provide accurate and authoritative information in regard to the subject matter covered. It is sold with the understanding that the publisher is not engaged in rendering legal, accounting, or other professional service. If legal advice or other assistance is required, the services of a competent professional person should be sought. *From a Declaration of Principles jointly adopted by a Committee of the American Bar Association and a Committee of Publishers.*

Library of Congress Cataloging-in-Publication Data

Paolo, Frank, 1950-
    How to make a great presentation in two hours!

    Includes indexes.
    ISBN 0-8119-0789-9
HF5718.22.P36   1993   93-19488
658.4'52--dc20   CIP

Manufactured in the United States of America

1 2 3 4 5 6 7 8 9 0

For Tracy. Forever.

TABLE OF CONTENTS

A NOTE ON LANGUAGE......................................viii

DEFINITIONS ix

HOW TO USE THIS BOOK xi

INTRODUCTION xiii

Section 1
The Two-Hour Formula

Step 1 - Choose one audience member 3

Step 2 - What do you want him to do or know? 3

Step 3 - Why should he do this?
or What do you want him to know? 4

Quick Review -...6

Step 4 - Create "Active" visual aids 6

Step 5 - Explain your points 8

Step 6 - Choose your opening 10

Step 7 - Choose your conclusion.................................12

Step 8 - Stop worrying 12

Step 9 - Rehearse out loud 14

Summary of Steps -...15

Section 2
The Formula Explained & Advanced Techniques

Step 1 - Choose one audience member 19
      Sample Introduction 35
      Summary...36

Step 2 - What do You want him to do or know? 39
      Summary...48

Step 3 - Why should he do this? or
      What do you want him to know? 49
      Summary...57
      Examples of Objectives and Supporting Points -58

Step 4 - Create "Active" visual aids 63
      Summary...70

What About Microphones? - 70

Step 5 - Explain your points 75
      Summary...83

Step 6 - Choose your opening 85
      Forget memorization! 89
      Raise your hand! 94
      Summary...100

Step 7 - Choose Your Conclusion 103
      Summary...113

Preview · Go Through · Review - 114

Step 8 - Stop worrying 119
      An anxiety-reducing strategy 139

Step 9 - Rehearse Out Loud 143
        Summary 154

Section 3
Miscellaneous

How will your Audience Judge You? 157

Dumb advice on presentations 162

Excuses   175

"I Am Joe's Audience" 178

The 10 Most Important Things to
Know About Presentations 183

A Letter to Corporate America 185

Jump! - (My "Closing" to this book.) 188

**A Quick Reference Guide
to 175 Presentation Ideas** - 195

About the Author 202

Index   204

A NOTE ON LANGUAGE

First, thorough readers might notice an occasional profane word which has slipped into the text. Please give these no attention. I must admit, I have been known to curse on very rare occasions when extreme circumstances necessitated that I use words from the English language which are not among its most noble. I hope any offended readers will take comfort in the fact that the words in question are quite mild when placed next to those which the editor has forced me to delete.

Second, our rich and wonderful English language has not, as of yet, developed a simple solution to the dilemma of sexist parlance. For expediency, throughout most of this book, I have used the traditional masculine pronoun to designate presenters of either sex. My choice is neither adequate nor creative. I apologize to any reader who takes offense at this selection.

DEFINITIONS

great - (grat') *adj*. 1. much above average.

average presentation - (av'-er-uj <u>prez-en-ta'-shun</u>) *noun*. 1. a common, dull method of dumping in an uninspired way too much unimportant information on people who are pretending to listen.

HOW TO USE THIS BOOK

If you only have a few hours before your presentation, immediately find a quiet room where you can speak out loud without being interrupted and turn to page 3. Completely follow the simple instructions on the next few pages without thinking too much about them. If you follow these steps just as they're written, I guarantee you will deliver a great presentation in two hours.

If you have more time, read the introduction on the next few pages for some background and then begin the same way as above. If you don't understand a specific step or would like to learn more about it, turn to the appropriate chapter in the reference section.

If you have an unlimited amount of time, read the entire book a few times and then do some volunteer work and exercise more. Better yet, write your own book on how to get an unlimited amount of time. I'd like to read it.

ACKNOWLEDGEMENTS

I always thought acknowledgement pages were dumb because I assumed the author was probably being unduly modest and I never knew any of the people on them anyway. Now, after writing a book, I can honestly say they are not dumb, I am not being modest when I say these people all contributed enormously to my efforts, and I know them all because they're my friends.

Thank you Frank Palazzolo, Marge Simcuski, Kathy Glenn, Pat Dengler, Tim Schapp, Dan Waffle, Patty Maher, Ginger Lynn Allen, Wes Fox, Lisa Sansone-Howell, Dr. Raymond Beard, Terry Hudson, Robin Watson, Robin Vining, and Chill Will.

A special thanks to all the kind people at Lifetime Books. I won't say this book would have been impossible without you but you've sure made it easier and a lot more fun.

INTRODUCTION

If you're like most people, you probably make dull presentations. I don't mean to be overly critical, and I'm sure you're a nice person, but there's a good chance that standing up before an audience delivering your ideas with clarity, authority, and excitement is neither one of your better skills nor your idea of a great time. You've got a lot of company. The best thing about most peoples' presentations is that they're probably worse than yours.

How do I know? Since you've picked up this book, you've shown you have an interest in presentations and improving your next one. I've also coached thousands of presenters over the years, listened to many more thousands of talks, and I know what passes for an average presentation. I know you can do a whole lot better than the average presenter. Trust me.

Most presentations are about as interesting as stale clams. Nervous presenters check their humanness at the door with their coats, hide behind podiums and dull visual aids, and then drone on too long with too much jumbled information. Excitement and creativity are rare. Fun is virtually unheard of. Audience members pretend they're listening (a skill learned in grade school) and are just thankful they aren't presenting that day. The most for which many presenters hope is to not make any horrible mistakes, blend in with the rest of the presenters, and then be forgotten quickly. Most get their wish.

A few brave ones try to liven up their talks with "ice breakers" from books with titles like "10,000,000 Sure-Fire Speech Starter Jokes." Of course these are usually people who couldn't tell two of their closest friends a joke over drinks without forgetting the punch line. When they try out their new material in a room filled with strangers, audience reaction is usually sympathy instead of laughter because if a joke is funny enough, relevant enough, and clean enough to tell an audience, chances are they've already heard it.

If there are a number of presenters lined up for the day, there's a good chance their opening will be exactly the same. It will probably be a stunner like, "good morning, ladies and gentlemen, my name is . . . .," or its creative variant, "good afternoon, ladies and gentlemen, my name is . . . .." If there's a microphone in the room, undoubtedly a few will blow into it and ask, "Can everyone hear me?" Unfortunately the answer is usually "yes."

There will probably be a few budding ophthalmologists flashing horrendous visual aids splattered with vast collections of numbers and diagrams asking, "Can everyone see this?" After realizing many can't, they mumble into a monotonal reading of that same dreary information immediately signaling audience members that the audio is going to be as dull as the visual. Again.

Do I exaggerate? Think of all the presentations you've heard in your life and divide them into two groups. In the first group include presentations in which you've been bored, confused, frustrated, thinking of other things, and anxious to hear them end. In the second group, include presentations that were exciting, persuasive, challenging, and fun.

I think you'll agree, the first group is more than a little larger than the second.

Why is the presentation situation so dreadful? In just about every other performance skill, there's a well-defined road to success. First you learn basic techniques, then you continually practice those techniques until you feel comfortable enough to be judged or to compete. The only exceptions to this process I can think of are making presentations and making love. Let's focus on the only one about which my wife thinks I know anything: making presentations.

Many people believe that if you can talk, you can present. Of course, many people believe just about anything. "If you can talk, you can present," is the intellectual equivalent of, "if you can write, you can write novels." Unfortunately, it just doesn't work that way.

But since so many people believe this nonsense, they think it's o.k. to push you out in front of an audience which is going to judge you even if you don't have basic skills, a great deal of practice, and a comfort level that will help guarantee your success. Is it any wonder most people dislike and fear making presentations?

Currently there are over 300 books and brochures in print on the general topic of public speaking. Virtually all of them spend a lot of time trying to make the reader a better presenter with all of the knowledge, skill, and dedication that takes.

Although many of these books are good for what they try to teach, I'm going to tell you an important secret: you really don't have to be a great presenter to deliver a great presentation.

Now I know speech coaches and instructors across the land probably just choked on that last thought and cursed my name to the heavens but it's true. Figure it out for yourself. In a few minutes you'll be introduced to a very simple formula for making a great presentation. It's so easy that in some cases you just fill in the blanks and use some words I give you. If you do exactly what I say, you'll be able to deliver a great presentation two hours from now. Your objective will be clear, your points concise and memorable, and the talk will be tailored to your specific audience. In other words, a "great" presentation.

Will making a great presentation make you a great presenter? Not by a good deal. Will it inspire you to learn more about presentations and aspire to be a great presenter? I hope so. Will it let you see that a lot of conventional wisdom about presentations is really conventional claptrap? Absolutely. Will making one great presentation turn your life around, provide you with knowledge and riches beyond your dreams, or I'll give you back the money you spent for this book? No.

You can use this book to make one great presentation by simply following the directions on the next few pages.

You can use it by reading the next few pages and the reference material that supports each point. With this book you can make one great presentation in a few hours or you can take much more time and learn how to become a great presenter. The information is here, the choice is yours.

Whichever you choose, I hope you'll think a lot, learn a lot, and have some fun between these pages. I'm honored that you've chosen me to help guide you to a great presentation.

Frank Paolo, 1993.

Section 1

THE TWO-HOUR FORMULA

Step 1
Choose one audience member
(5 minutes)

• If you have more than two hours for your presentation and would like to know the background for choosing one audience member, please turn to page 19.

• Close your eyes and imagine yourself in front of your audience. Now pick one representative audience member or the most important audience member; whoever is more appropriate for your presentation.

• A representative audience member is a real person who's an average audience member. This is not a person who will completely agree or disagree with what you have to say but will listen to your presentation (one hopes) with an open mind. This person will represent your entire audience.

• If you choose the most important audience member, that person and why you chose him or her should be obvious.

• Now at the top of a piece of paper, write that person's name or identify him or her in a memorable way.

Examples: "Joan Doe" or "President of Company"

Step 2

What do you want him to do or know?
(10 minutes)

• This is one of the most important steps in the formula. It's the objective of the presentation. If you'd like more information on this step, please turn to page 39.

• Imagine the person you chose in Step 1 sitting across from you right now. Then, right below the name or description you've written on your paper, write and complete the following sentence:

"I want you to:_____ (Examples: buy my company's telecommunication's equipment, know about the telecommunication's automatic beeping system.)"

• Remember: this must be one, clear, simple sentence. Don't complicate your presentation. Simplify! You can only have one objective per presentation. If you absolutely must have more than one objective, divide the presentation into distinct sections and think of each section as an individual presentation.

• When you have your simple sentence written, stand up and say it loudly. Say it twice as loud as you normally speak! Say it this loud at least five times.

WARNING: Dull Presenters Beware!

• Are you thinking of skipping Step 2 because you think you'll feel foolish talking out loud by yourself? Uh-oh. Be careful. If you start completing only the steps with which you feel comfortable, you'll end up with a comfortably dull presentation. All great presenters talk to themselves. They call it rehearsal. It won't hurt a bit and it will help you a lot.

• Decide right now if you are going to deliver a great presentation or an instantly forgettable one. If you decide to deliver a great presentation and have not completed Step 2, stand up right now and do it!

Step 3
Why should he do this?
or, What things do you want him to know?
(10 minutes)

• This is a hard step for mediocre presenters because they have such a terrible time simplifying. But it's critical! (Reference for Step 3: page 49.)

• Tell your chosen audience member why he should do what you ask (from Step 2) with only two reasons - each limited to only two or three words. If you want him to know something (again from Step 2) limit what you want him to know listing only two important elements - each limited to only two or three words.

• Let's look at the examples first to see that this sounds harder than it really is.

'I want you to do this' example: "You should buy my telecommunications system for two basic reasons: 1. cost-effectivness, and 2. life-time guarantee."

'I want you to know something' example: "In this presentation, I'd like you to learn about the two most important responsibilities of my job: 1. managing people, and 2. managing time."

• For more examples of Steps 2 and 3 combined, please see page 58.

• Now it's your turn. Take the page on which you've already written the first two steps and write just two points - each limited to two or three words.

• My two major points are:

      1._____ _____
      2._____ _____

• Important: NUMBER the points (reference page 52). Now stand up and repeat Steps 2 and 3 together (saying the numbers also) twice as loud as you normally speak. Imagine your chosen audience member. Look right at him (in your mind as you're standing) and repeat these words and numbers at least five times. (Imagine the surprised look on his face when he realizes that this is not going to be a typical, meandering presentation.)

NOTE: After this page, I'm only going to use the persuasive (Why should he do this?) example for simplicity. If you have an informative (What do you want him to know?) presentation, please know all of the following steps still apply and you actually have an easier presentation to deliver.

Quick Review
(3 minutes)

• Let's quickly review your objective and two main supporting points, each limited to two or three key words. Stand up and fill in the blanks out loud.

This should be easy.

"I want you to (do something)_____
for two main reasons, number one: _____
and number two: _____."
or

"I want you to (know something) about_____.
It has two major elements, number one: _____ and number two: _____."

• Now stand up again (I know you sat down again) and repeat this sentence twice as loud as you normally speak.

• Are you having any difficulty? If you are, it's probably because you're trying to make the exercise too complicated. It should be very easy if you've completed steps 2 and 3. If you're having trouble with simplicity, imagine the trouble your audience is going to have trying to understand you! Simplify—especially at this point.

• Now let's go to step 4 to see how simple visual aids can be.

Step 4
Create "active" visual aids
(10 minutes)

• Visual aids do not have to be large, electronically-enhanced, expensive pieces of art. Colorful slides and overheads are nice if you've got the time and money but they also have significant disadvantages. (Reference: page 63)

• Some of the best visual aids are the simplest because they demand that audience members interact with your presentation. The best way for audience members to interact is taking notes from an outlined structure you provide.

• Here's some news that's even better: most of your "active" visual aids have already been written and are waiting to be copied. What should they "say?"

• your objective,

• your two or three "key" points (numbered, always numbered!)

• lots of white space, and

• (if you want to be really fancy) a title.

• Below you will find an example of an "active" visual aid (taken from Step 2). When you put your presentation into this simple format, please have enough copies made for each audience member and another for yourself.

• Hand out these sheets or have someone else hand them out at the very beginning of your presentation. Then while you're launching into your opening (a very nervous time for most presenters) audience members are momentarily distracted with this impressive "visual aid" relieving you of some of the pressure.

"Selecting the Telecommunications System that's Right for You"

OBJECTIVE : To have you consider the key reasons why you should purchase the Global Communications system.

KEY REASONS
1. Cost Effectiveness:

2. Lifetime Guarantee:

Step 5
Explain your points
(20 minutes)

Danger: too much information!

• Most inexperienced presenters dump too much information in a disorganized jumble on the intellectual laps of bored audience members. They think, "it can't hurt; I must cover it all!" They're wrong. It does hurt. If an audience member is bored listening to information that doesn't apply to his needs, he tunes out. And all that "must cover" information impotently flops around the room. (Reference: page 75.)

• Then guess what happens when you get to a point that's critical to an audience member? That's right; he's not listening.

• How do you know which details are critical to your audience members? First, accept the hard fact you'll never know for sure so just do your best and present too little information rather than too much. (Now I know these last words were shocking to most inexperienced presenters but it's one of the key reasons their presentations are usually dull.)

• Here's a fact good presenters know: if you present too little information in an exciting way, audience members will usually ask you for more in a Question and Answer period; but if you present too much, they'll stop listening, look forward to the end of your presentation, and will be reluctant to ask questions for fear of being bored to death again!

Now. . . .
1. Take one of your Visual Aid copies and a pen (from Step 4).
2. Imagine your chosen audience member (from Step 1) and
3. Tell him (in your mind, of course) only the most important details that support your points.

4. Write out these details in a "bullet" format. ("Bullet" means only write key words - DO NOT WRITE OUT COMPLETE SENTENCES!)
5. Remember: err on the side of simplicity.
6. Refer to the following example.
7. Do not rehearse the "body" of your presentation just yet.

"Selecting the Telecommunications System that's Right for You"

OBJECTIVE : To have you consider the key reasons why you should purchase the Global Communications system.

KEY REASONS

1. Cost Effectiveness:
   · over a three-year period, cheaper than any major competitor
   · unique lease and paper-supply guarantee (explain)
   · free installation and hardware maintenance (leave copies of warranty before leaving)
   · special software with inexpensive training package (explain)

2. Lifetime Guarantee:
   · "worry-free" guarantee (explain)
   · no competitor makes same claim
   · "for as long as you own this company, you won't have to worry about your telecommunication system"

A Note on Notes:

- Please don't confuse the "bulletted point" outlined on the previous page for the "active" visual aids you're going to pass out to audience members. There should be only one copy of the previous page and that's for you to use as notes (if you need them).
- And please don't add any more information to your notes! The more words you write down, the more you'll be tempted to look down and read rather than deliver your presentation. If you're just going to write out your presentation and read it, you're slipping back into the pits of presentation mediocrity. Some audiences like being read to: preschoolers and others who can't read. But a grown up audience is waiting to hear you deliver your presentation. Don't let them down.

Step 6
Choose your opening
(10 minutes)

- "Good morning, ladies and gentlemen. My name is _____" is one of the most common and worst openings presenters deliver (Reference: page 85.)
- There are many better openings (Reference: page 91) but assuming you have a very limited amount of time for your presentation, the best opening is a strong, clear statement of your objective from Step 2 and your points from Step 3.
- Combined with a quick, "pat" phrase (I'll give you two in a moment) these two steps will be the first words out of your mouth in front of an audience.
- Do not say "good morning." Do not say "what an honor it is for me blah, blah" (who cares?) Do not tell a joke (are you Jay Leno?)

Just say,

"In the next few minutes, I'm going to" (a combination of Steps 2 and 3).

or

"In this presentation, I'm going to" (a combination of Steps 2 and 3).

Example:

• "In the next few minutes, I'm going to ask you to consider purchasing the Global Communications system for two specific reasons: number one, cost effectiveness and number two, its lifetime guarantee."

• Now, using one of these standard phrases, write on your paper: the phrase and Steps 2 and 3 just like the example (and literally write "number one" and "number two").

• Stand up, imagine your audience, and loudly say this sentence again and again until it is completely memorized. This is the only part of a presentation for which I suggest literal memorization.

WARNING: Are We Sliding into Dullness?

• Just now, did you just memorize your opening "in your mind" without standing and rehearsing it aloud? C'mon now! Your audience members aren't mind readers. They'll want to hear your voice. Going over the material again and again out loud is going to make you feel comfortable with it. If you hear your opening for the first time along with your audience members, know you've probably slid into the pit of presentation mediocrity.

• Crawl out! Crawl out now! You can make it! If you haven't delivered your opening aloud - do it now. Loudly and proudly. Again and again. And don't look down at those other poor presenters wallowing in yawning dullness. There, but for the Grace of God, you could have wallowed.

Step 7
Choose your conclusion
(10 minutes)

• If you're like most so-so presenters, you probably end your presentation with a mumbled "thank you." "Thank you" (of course) is one of the dullest ways you can conclude for many reasons (Reference: page 103). What you're really saying is "thank you for sitting through my less-than-interesting presentation."

• The good news is you already have a much better ending - and it's even written out!

• Simply take your opening (Step 6) and a few "pat" words (provided shortly) and you have a conclusion that's superior to most.

Here's our example:

• "So for those two reasons, number one, cost effectiveness and number two, its lifetime guarantee, I'd like you to consider purchasing the Global Communications system. (Pause)   Any questions?"

• Now it's your turn. On your sheet, write out your conclusion based on the example above, stand up, and say it out loud (twice as loud as you normally speak) until you're comfortable with it.

• You've now only used about an hour and one-half of your time (assuming you did not have the time nor the inclination to look up references.) You're almost ready to begin the single most important element which will separate you from common presenters - rehearsing out loud. But first, let's stop worrying.

Step 8
Stop worrying
(5 minutes)

What! Me Worry?

• Of course you're worrying; most presenters do. In the thousands of presenters I've coached, only a very few have not worried (and they should have - a few were so bad, I began worrying about why they weren't worrying!)

Here are some things you should know:

• Right now, you don't have enough time to learn how not to be afraid of presentations assuming you're going to speak very shortly. However, if you do have the time (and certainly before your next presentation) please turn to the excellent anxiety-reducing techniques beginning on page 119.

• Since you probably don't have enough time to learn how not to be afraid, the only one thing you can do at this point is pretend. That's right! You're going to act like you're not afraid. How?

1.   DO NOT speak about your nervousness to anyone before the presentation. Do not apologize for it, explain it, or make a joke about it. If someone asks you if you're nervous, smile, and tell him "no, I'm excited" - and watch the look on his face.

2.   During your presentation speak TWICE AS LOUD as you normally speak. You've already been rehearsing this. Although you'll feel as if you're shouting, audience members usually interpret loud, projecting presenters as confident and commanding. Trust me on this one - speak TWICE AS LOUD - and you'll be surprised at the result!

3.   Have Confidence in your presentation. If you've completed the previous steps, you're getting ready to deliver a great presentation! The audience will be impressed by its simplicity and structure and surprised that you're so distinctively different in a professional way.

4.   Think of this presentation in terms of relative importance. When you're 93 years old and lying on your death-bed reminiscing about the great events of your life, how high on the list do you think this presentation will be?

Now, let's continue rehearsing (and don't you dare fake this!)

Step 9
Rehearse out loud
(20 minutes)

This may well be the most important exercise in your presentation. If you have the time, learn the best methods of rehearsal (Reference: page 143). If you don't have time, just follow these guidelines:

• Assume you, or someone you've chosen, has already passed out to your audience your "active" visual aids. (I suggest this be done for your "real" presentation.

• Now stand up and put your copy of your "bulleted-points" outline on the table in front of you. These are not to be read but only referred to if you happen to forget a point for more than a second or two.

• Visualize your audience in front of you, pause, smile, and then state your memorized opening in a twice-as-loud-as-you-normally-speak voice.("In the next few minutes . . .") If you have difficulty remembering your opening, go back to Step 6.

• Then, in the same loud, commanding voice start going over your points just as you'll do "for real" in your presentation.

• Think it through as you speak. Take your time. You already know most of what you're going to say. You've already said much of this out loud a number of times already. Keep speaking. Loudly and with authority.

• Don't keep referring to your notes. Instead, think as you speak and try to establish eye contact with your visualized audience. Keep speaking.

• Make a mistake? Shrug your shoulders, smile, and go on. This isn't a heart transplant operation! Nor is it a test to see if you can remember every single word. It's communication - the best presenters get their ideas across simply and clearly; and they often forget words or phrases. How come you never noticed this as an audience member? Because you were listening to strong, simple ideas presented with authority. Your audience is going to notice the same thing.

SUMMARY OF STEPS

STEP 1
Choose one audience member
(5 minutes)

Step 2
What do you want him to do or know?
(10 minutes)

Step 3
Why should he do this?
(10 minutes)

Step 4
Create "Active" visual aids
(10 minutes)

Step 5
Explain your points
(20 minutes)

Step 6
Choose your opening
(10 minutes)

Step 7
Choose your conclusion
(10 minutes)

Step 8
Stop worrying
(5 minutes)

Step 9
Rehearse out loud
(20 minutes)

Section 2

**THE FORMULA EXPLAINED &
ADVANCED TECHNIQUES**

STEP 1
CHOOSE ONE
AUDIENCE MEMBER

Tailoring your presentation for an individual audience is one of the most important things you can do to make it successful. Common presenters begin with the premise "what do I want to tell these people?" Good presenters begin by asking "what do these people want to hear from me?" This section covers different aspects of audience analysis and explains why it's often best to think of just one person when you're creating a presentation.

Why do I choose one person when I create my presentation?

An audience is composed of many different people. If you try to create your talk thinking of all these people and each of their different needs and attention spans and likes and dislikes, you're going to crash before you begin. Good presenters focus on only one person while creating the presentation; either the most important "decision-maker" in the group or a "representative" audience member.

Who is the "most important" audience member?

This person is easiest to define when thinking of an audience. He or she is usually the highest ranking officer of a company, the person who will decide the outcome of the presentation, or the person with the most power in the room. New presenters constantly strive to please everyone in their presentations from this "most important" audience member to those who aren't even listening. This "shotgun approach" is a mistake. It usually dilutes your message so much that the whole audience drowns in blandness.

Who is a "representative" audience member?

If you have many "important" people in your audience (or none) you must choose a "representative" audience member. This is a little tricky but still worth doing. A "representative" audience member must represent the majority of your audience.

This person has not made up his mind one way or the other and will really listen to your presentation before making a decision or learning about the subject matter.

Think of your audience as represented by a bell curve. On one side are a few people who are behind you 100 percent. These people will support your presentation and back your ideas no matter what you say. If you completely blank out during your talk or start speaking in tongues, they'll still applaud madly when you conclude and congratulate you on a job well done. Don't waste your speech on these people. "Preaching to the converted" is a real waste of time unless you're going to pass a collection plate when you're finished.

On the other side of the curve are those few individuals who would not accept your ideas if they were preapproved by God himself. Maybe they have a grudge against you or your company or maybe they're presenting competing ideas but in any case, no matter what you say or do, they're not going to support your presentation. Ignore these people when creating your speech!

Too many times I help executives prepare presentations and they say, "Well, I must include point X because Joe Horror will stand up and call me a rotten worm if I don't." I then ask if Joe Horror represents the majority of the audience or if the rest of the audience cares at all about point

X. "Of course not," replies the executive, "but that's his area of expertise and he always tries to make me look bad on it."

"Well," I reply, "in all the times you've slanted your presentation for his benefit, how many times has it succeeded in shutting him up?" You can guess what I'm told. What's not so clear is that slanting presentations to nonrepresentative individuals (whom you can't convince anyway) or including points interesting to only a select few is not only a waste of time - it's sabotaging your objective with the rest of the audience.

The people you really can convince are the vast majority represented by the largest section of the audience bell curve. If they continually "tune out" of your talk while you're trying to placate the "Joe Horrors" of the world, you can hardly expect them to "tune in" when you're speaking to them. Please remember, it's not an audience's job to listen; it's a presenter's job to make them want to listen.

What should I know about my one audience member?

The easy answer is "as much as you can." What most people consider a presentation is composed of three elements: the presenter (you), the "presentation" (the ideas or point of view to be expressed), and those present (audience members). Out of the three, the audience is certainly the most important. If it wasn't for audience members, there would be no reason to create and deliver a presentation. Despite this fact, few presenters consider audience members at all until they stand before them.

If you have the time, here's a short list of questions to ask yourself about your chosen audience member before proceeding to the next steps of the formula. You can probably think of many more that are specific to your situation.

- What does he now know about my subject?
- How does he feel about it?

- What arguments might persuade him to my point of view?
- Has he considered this before?
- What information does he need to make a decision?
- When can he make a decision?
- Is he detail oriented or concept oriented?
- What questions might he ask?

The more you can learn about your audience member, the better your chance of delivering an effective presentation keyed specifically to his needs. If you're even moderately successful at this, you'll be far more compelling than the vast majority of common presenters.

Why do I imagine this audience member "seated across from me"?

The first time most presenters even consider audience members is when they face them in the presentation. To an actor, this is the awful equivalent of "rehearsing in public" - something a good actor would never do. The shock of seeing real, live faces politely anticipating a presentation is enough to skyrocket the blood pressure of all but the most experienced presenters.

The more times you can meet and face audience members, even if it's only in your mind, the more relaxed you'll be when the actual encounter occurs.

Why do audience members make me so nervous?

Well they don't, of course. You make yourself nervous by not thinking rationally about them before your presentation. Presenters are audience members many more times than they are presenters. You forget that as an audience member you don't sit there thinking horrible thoughts about the presenter (in most cases). Why do you assume your audience is thinking horrible thoughts about you?

For a thorough discussion about presentation anxiety and what you can do about it, please turn to page 119.

For a lighter look at how audiences view presenters, you may wish to read my article, "I Am Joe's Audience" on page 178.

What if there's a wide gap of knowledge in my audience?

This is one of the toughest problems presenters have to face because there really are no good solutions to it. If you present your message assuming audience members have a high level of knowledge and they don't, they become confused and often stop listening. But if you present your message by first bringing everyone up to speed, the audience members who already know the material become bored and stop listening.

How many times do we hear, "I know many of you have heard this stuff before but for those who haven't, I'll go over it again." These presenters might as well present blankets and pillows to audience members who might well appreciate a nap instead of listening to a dull drone of previously learned material. So what can you do? There are a number of different strategies but no one is perfect. Choose the one that best fits your situation.

- Strategy 1: Different presentations. Although this is a lot more work, it's often worth dividing the audience into different groups for the specific purpose of educating the one with less knowledge. You may even have a mini-talk to bring that group up to speed and afterwards deliver a full blown presentation to the entire reassembled group. Of course, everyone should know why this is taking place and be reminded that you were thoughtful enough to consider their needs.

• <u>Strategy 2:   Prepresentation Reading:</u>   I like prepresentation reading. It's an excellent way to deliver the background knowledge necessary for an understanding of your presentation without boring to death people who already know it. Prepresentation reading should be short, easy-to-read information with the stated purpose of providing sufficient background to understand your presentation. It should be delivered to audience members a day or two before your talk.

"But what if they don't read it!?" I hear some of my seminar people complain. Tough. You've lived up to your responsibility as a good presenter by providing the material for your audience's benefit. If they choose not to enlighten themselves with it, there's really nothing more you can do.

Another point on prepresentation reading is that it should clearly state the objective of the presentation. If audience members and presenters don't agree on this objective, it's just not going to go well for you regardless of what you say and how well you say it.

• <u>Strategy 3: Postpresentation Reading.</u> This is sometimes appropriate when you know your audience particularly well and they trust you. You say, in effect, "I don't want to take the time at this point in my presentation to explain point X because many of you already know it but I will distribute a complete written explanation of it at the end of my talk for those of you who don't."

It's important to make sure you distribute this at the end of your talk; not at the beginning, not during,

- no matter how much audience members beg or plead. This is true for virtually all handouts except for the one I suggest in my presentation formula.

As you might imagine, there's a very good reason for this. When you give audience members something to read during your presentation, you've given them a grand choice between two presentations: yours and the one on printed sheets before them. Since it's often easier and more pleasant for audience members to read rather than listen to most presenters, I'm afraid your presentation might finish in second place. It's tough enough to focus an audience's attention on your message without providing attractive diversions.

Strategy 4: (as a last resort) Aim High. If you really can't (or won't) bridge the knowledge gap between audience members with the strategies I've suggested, your best bet is to "aim high" and assume they know more than they do. It's always better to have audience members listening for information (even if they don't understand it completely) than to have them tune out because they've heard it before. Also, if you've made your presentation exciting enough, they may even ask for further explanations in the Question and Answer Period.

How can I learn what my audience member likes?

The same way you learn what your lover likes. Ask her! (or him.) There are a number of indirect ways such as asking people who've presented to him before or people who know what he likes, but the direct method is almost always the best. Most audience members are flattered they will receive a personalized presentation rather than a warmed over version of the usual canned chatter.

How can I tell if my audience member is concept or detail oriented?

Although no one is strictly one way or the other, it's important to know if your audience member strongly favors one approach. It's also important for you to know that good oral presentations are better for concepts than for details. Now this doesn't mean that details aren't important in presentations, it just means it's usually better to present strong concepts out loud and support them with a few details. If more details are needed they should be presented in another way perhaps written and distributed after your presentation. For a thorough look at just how much detail to include in presentations, please turn to page 75.

Certain audience "types" usually favor one approach over the other. Although these are stereotypical examples (and might not apply to your specific audience) here are some general guidelines:

- <u>Management</u> in business is usually concept oriented. Think of management cliches: "the big picture," "the bottom line." Good managers can't get bogged down in details because if they did, they couldn't move quickly enough.

- <u>Technically based people</u> are inevitably detail oriented. Think of a cliche that pertains to them: "when I ask them what time it is, they tell me how to build a watch." Technically oriented people love details. They dump pounds of them on audience members. If the audience is filled with other technically oriented people, everyone has a good time. If the audience isn't, people spend a lot of time looking at their watches and wondering when the presentation will end.

• The general public is usually concept oriented. Too many details often confuse them. Raised in a culture where much of their information comes from 30-second commercial messages and news "sound bites," most people are overwhelmed by details and begin to distrust speakers who use too many.

What else should I consider about my one audience member?

One of the most important things is his perception of you. Inexperienced presenters don't realize their presentations start long before the first words tumble out of their mouths. Their presentations actually begin as soon as audience members see them and instantly make value judgments about them.

When an audience member sees a presenter, many questions race through his mind probably at a subconscious level. He's asking himself, "Does this person really know what he's talking about?", "Is he going to try to take me for a ride?", "Can I trust him?", "Why did he wear such an ugly tie?" He also is registering what I call, non-controllable perceptions: is the presenter a woman or a man? Is the presenter old or young? Inexperienced or experienced? Does he look confident or like he just shoplifted something?

The answers to all of these questions (and many more) tremendously influence the way an audience member listens to your presentation. I wish this wasn't true. I wish audience members really could objectively judge the merits of your presentation based solely on your intelligence, logic, creativity, humanness, and the soundness of your ideas. But they don't. Very often crucial value judgments of your presentation are made by audience members based on superficial evaluations of you!

How can I shape my audience member's impression of me?

One of the fastest ways your audience member makes an evaluation of you is by how you dress. Once again, please don't confuse the messenger with the message. I'm not saying this is right; I'm just saying it happens all the time. A general rule for presentation dressing is, "if someone remembers what you wore, you've probably dressed incorrectly." One of my suggestions to my seminar presenters is, "dress one step above your audience members." If they dress without ties, you wear a tie without a jacket. If they dress with ties, you wear a tie and a jacket. If they wear ties and jackets, you wear a suit. Of course if they all wear suits, you do too. And button the jacket.

In the business world, one thing presenters forget is that clothing is not an expression of personal identity. Indeed, it's often just the opposite. Clothing in many corporations is an expression of team identity. Don't forget that most large companies were started and continue to be run by teams of dedicated men. The background of their clothing ideas come from the uniforms of team sports and the military - certainly no bastions of individual expression in attire.

Clothing conformity is spectacularly apparent in presentations. We expect to see management presenters deliver their talks in traditional business suits, clean shirts, and instantly forgettable ties. Although you may be able to think of a few exceptions to this, I'd suggest that the fact you remember those presenters underscores that they are the exceptions rather than the rule.

How important is the "corporate uniform" in a presentation? A few years ago I was invited to a sales meeting of a company in which I coached a number of executives. It was a hot August day in a large Eastern city and the hotel air conditioning wasn't working well. As the executives and I trudged past the reception table, we were handed typical meeting packets along with blue t-shirts emblazoned with the meeting's theme.

Entering the crowded auditorium, I saw an ocean of these t-shirts on the 1500 or so meeting participants. In a few minutes, there was a flutter at the door as the chief executive officer (whom I had not coached) and his assistants walked in, packets and t-shirts in hand. I was immediately struck by the situation facing the CEO. Did he maintain authority in his "corporate uniform" of a $2000 well-tailored pinstripe suit in the stifling auditorium? Or did he take off his suit jacket, slip on the t-shirt, and show he was "one of the boys"?

His answer didn't surprise me. Without hesitation he took off his jacket, slipped on the t-shirt, and put his jacket right back on!

This gentleman was certainly "one of the boys" - but he was also their leader. No one was going to forget that during his presentation by the way he was (or wasn't) dressed regardless of the temperature of the room.

Women should dress even more conservatively than men. Remember, this is not an exercise in equal rights or "what should be" - this is a technique to positively influence your audience's perception of you for your advantage.

Although these clothing "rules" aren't as strict outside of the business world, the same ideas apply. If you have a doubt on what to wear as a presenter, it's always better to be over-dressed rather than under-dressed. Even members of the American Sunbathing Association Board of Directors (nudists) wear traditional clothing to many of their meetings. If they can make this sacrifice, so can you!

Why should I dress up to present when no one else does?

And if Johnny jumped off the roof could we expect you to land on top of him? One of the ways you can favorably impress your target audience member is not to be just like all the other dull presenters he's heard for years. To be "distinctively different in a professional way" will only enhance your credibility. Too many presenters try to relax themselves about their talks by saying in effect, "This isn't really a formal presentation, this is just a conversation where I stand up." When they present their ideas with this lackluster thinking, it's no wonder few people listen and fewer still remember what they've said.

Can the correct clothing "make" the presenter? Of course not. It's just one way to help shape your audience member's critical first impression of you. I know I'd find it difficult to communicate an important message if my chosen audience member sat there and wondered why I wore such an ugly tie.

Besides dress, what's another way I can favorably impress my audience member before the presentation?

Your attitude. Some speakers trudge into the room in which they'll present like condemned prisoners before the guillotine. They hang their heads, wring their hands, and drain their faces of any last signs of life as they remember it.

Others show their nervousness by noisily chirping how much they hate making presentations, chat endlessly about their visual aids or their unfamiliarity with the talk, or launch into unceasing stories about anything and nothing to delay the inevitable.

Although audience members may appear sympathetic, they must also begin to wonder why this strange person was invited to speak in the first place. Certainly the presenter's credibility (and the audience's tolerance) suffer. And you must believe that this influences how the audience listens to the presentation.

A good presenter knows that his presentation begins as soon as any audience member sees him before he starts to speak. He appears relaxed and confident - even if he's not. (For more information on this, see Chapter 8.) He does not speak about his presentation except in positive terms. He does not joke about it, discuss the mechanics of it, or apologize for it - ever. If some misguided audience member asks, "Are you nervous?", a good presenter looks him straight in the eye and says, "No, I'm excited!"

He appears authoritative in a respectful way. Before the presentation if someone asks him if he would prefer the room set up in a "classroom" or "horseshoe" manner, he does not grovel and mumble, "oooh, whatever's best for you." He quickly chooses one even if the choice has never occurred to him before in his life.

In other words, the presenter begins his presentation before he starts to speak by presenting an attitude of "I'm a competent professional who knows what he's doing and I have some valuable ideas to deliver. It will be to your benefit to listen."

All right — I'm properly dressed and have the right attitude. What else can I do to favorably impress my audience member?

Show some life and enthusiasm about your chance to present that day and your subject matter! Your audience member will be definitely unfair on this issue. If you are enthused about your presentation, your audience member might become that way. But it never works in reverse. I've never seen anyone present as if he's auditioning for a bit part in a zombie movie and then watch audience members burst into spontaneous excitement.

As a matter of fact, there's probably no better way to sap an audience's energy than to be a mopey, hand-wringing presenter. A few years ago, a large client of mine was introducing a major new product. The people who worked for the company were excited about its possibilities because they knew it was radically different than anything in their highly competitive marketplace.

On a special night, the employees were invited to a gala "product reveal" in the large company auditorium. When I arrived, I noticed people were excited with anticipation. They talked a lot, were smiling at their co-workers, and waved to friends across the hall. When the president of the company was introduced, there was thunderous applause as he walk to the podium.

"Good evening, ladies and gentlemen," he read from his script in dull, flat, gloom-filled tones, "Welcome to one of the most exciting points in our company's life."

In minutes the enthusiasm of the audience began to trickle away. Within ten minutes there were audible signs of boredom but the president didn't even seem to notice. Rarely looking up, he continued to read his script like it was a list of ingredients on a box of oatmeal he didn't want to eat. His lack of presentation "life" sapped the audience's enthusiasm for the presentation and, some would say, even for the product itself.

But what if I'm not enthused about the material I'm presenting?

The terrible truth about the matter is that most material most people present most of the time will only be exciting if they make it that way. That's just the way it is. But that doesn't mean you have to convey that to the people in your audience. Those people are looking to you to generate some excitement in their souls.

How can I do that if I'm not excited?

If you're not enthused about your chance to present or the subject matter in your presentation, there's only one thing you can do (and they tell me women do this better than men): FAKE IT! That's right, FAKE IT! Look, if you're not enthused about your opportunity, and we know audience members won't become enthused about it if you're not, and you must give the presentation, what else can you do?

Isn't that unethical?

No, it's unethical to deliver a presentation for your company or your organization or yourself and sabotage it with daggers of dullness. It's unethical to make audience members sit through a bland drone of presentation pollution because you can't get up enough excitement to make it interesting or fun. Of course, if you really have some moral qualms about your presentation, that's another issue. In that case, you probably shouldn't be presenting it at all. But in most instances you have the responsibility to generate excitement in audience members.

How do I show enthusiasm if I don't feel it?

There are two vital ways I discuss in depth later in the book. That's where I talk more about your actual presentation style. For now, just know that showing enthusiasm for your chance to present and your subject matter is one way to favorably impress your audience before your presentation.

Anything else?

A proper introduction is a great opportunity of which few inexperienced presenters take advantage. Remember what you're doing here. You're trying to favorably win your target audience member over before you even begin your presentation. A well-written introduction, although not appropriate for every presentation, is an excellent way to build your credibility.

As a professional speaker, I know how important a good introduction is and I know I'll receive a good one every time

I speak. My intro talks about my experience in presentations, the prestigious clients I've had the honor to serve, my education, awards, and the professional articles I've written. It's concise, easily read and understood, and builds a great deal of credibility with my audience. Most of it is true.

I know my introduction will always be good because I wrote it myself. And I wasn't too modest either. Long ago I learned that if you trust this vital piece of your presentation to the people running the meeting, it will receive little attention and no priority. In a large meeting, even if you're the main speaker, your introduction will fall somewhere between 'flowers on the table' and 'who tips bus people?' on the list of what's important.

How should my introduction be written?

Your introduction should include any material that will help you immediately build audience credibility. Specifically: education, experience, awards, and any respectable publications for which you've written. It should also contain the phonetic (fo-NEH-tic) pronunciation of any difficult words - especially your name.

It should be printed or typed, have easy to read words, and it should probably be in 18-point type if you can arrange that. It should not be any longer than one page, double-spaced.

My introduction on the next page is humbly offered as a simple yet wonderful example of what your introduction could be like.

Is there anything I should not include in my introduction?

Lots of things; in fact, just about everything I didn't include above. Cute or funny stories usually don't help with audience credibility. References to spouses, children, hobbies, and pets can also be quickly eliminated. If you're delivering a presentation on advanced instrumentation theory, the fact that you have two children (ages four and seven) isn't going to help your credibility one iota.

Once I have my introduction written, who should deliver it?

Simply, the person who can help build audience credibility the most - usually the "power" person in the room or the person who is responsible for the meeting. When speaking before a large group, I bring my introduction to the "ranking" company executive, show him that it's all written out, and ask him to read it for me. I also tell him he's free to change it any way he wishes. Of course, he almost never does. Then, when he's reading my less-than-modest introduction, part of his audience credibility is shared with me before I even begin to speak.

Presentations I give are too casual for an introduction.

You might be right. However, if you don't have a good introduction and constantly look for opportunities to use it, you may end up being relegated to that great gray morass of dull presenters.

You'll never know for sure exactly what's "right" for every presentation but you've got to start taking some risks or everything's going to remain in it's same yawning state. Erring on the side of professionalism isn't such a bad way to go.

Introduction Example:
Frank Paolo (PAUL - o) has been making great presentations for a long time. In 1972 he was officially ranked as the number two collegiate speaker in the nation. Shortly after graduation,

he joined a large advertising and public relations agency writing copy and speeches for business executives. He quickly knew that delivering presentations was not necessarily a strong point of most executives (to put it kindly) so he began to coach them and became the agency's first Director of Presentation Services.

In 1981, Mr. Paolo began his own consulting business. Since that time he has coached over 3000 business people in his seminars, written speeches for and coached a large number of corporate executives, and made presentations to many more on the professional lecture circuit. His articles on business presentations have appeared in *Meetings & Conventions* magazine and many corporate newsletters.

Mr. Paolo's clients include Eastman Kodak Company, Bausch & Lomb, Bank Marketers of America, Fairchild Systems, Mobil Chemical Company, Holman Agency of Toronto, General Electric, Corning Glass, Young & Rubicam, and Xerox Corporation among others.

His presentations and seminars have taken him across the United States and as far north as Calgary, Alberta and as far south as San Paulo, Brazil.

Summary

Choosing one audience member before making your presentation makes a lot of sense. The chosen person should be either "the most important" person in your audience or a "representative" audience member. Choose well; you will create and rehearse your entire presentation with this person in mind.

One advantage good presenters have is that they know their presentations actually begin in the minds of audience members long in advance of their talks. Although there are certain "non-controllable" factors involved which will affect how an audience member listens to your talk (such as if you are young or old), there are many other factors you can control. Among these: how you dress, how confident and enthusiastic you act, and if you have an introduction that immediately helps build credibility.

Most presenters think they are merely messengers of presentation information. They think audience members will only objectively listen to facts and the logic of their points and not be influenced by superficial attributes such as dress or attitude. Of course, most presenters think a lot of strange things about presentations and their "presentation reality" should be severely examined before it is dismissed completely.

In short, choose one audience member and then do everything you can to tailor your presentation and his perception of you to your benefit.

STEP 2
WHAT DO YOU WANT HIM TO DO OR KNOW?

After you've selected your chosen audience member, you must then ask yourself the question, "what do I want him to do or know?" This is the objective step of your presentation and it's absolutely critical. If don't have a good objective, you won't have a great presentation. Period. Objectives are the keystones of presentations. If they are unclear, misunderstood, or come in small bunches like grapes ("I have three objectives for my five-minute presentation"), then the foundation of your presentation is going to crumble and the eyes of your audience member are going to glaze.

Let me make a distinction here between "want him to do" and "want him to know" presentations. "Want him to do" involves an action you want an audience member to take. We sometimes refer to these as *persuasive* presentations. Since these are more challenging and more common than "want him to know" or *informative* presentations, I've used them for most of the examples in this book.

All sales talks are "want him to do" presentations ("buy this"). Most instructive lectures are "want him to know" presentations ("learn this"). Of course, there are those former philosophy majors who contend that all presentations are really persuasive presentations because you must convince someone to learn something. Ignore these people or tell them to go back to their park benches and sit down. Thank you.

Your presentation objective should be one, simple, concise statement that answers the question on the top of this page. "To convince him to buy my telecommunications system," is an example of a good objective. "To convince him that we're a good company that sells superior telecommunications systems any one of which could successfully meet his needs, increase his bottom line, and provide wealth and peace of mind to the vast majority of his living employees," is not.

Why are you so strict about my presentation objective?

It's impossible for you to create and deliver a great presentation without a strong presentation objective. Having a clear objective won't guarantee a great presentation but not having one will guarantee a lousy presentation. A strong objective is the foundation of your presentation. Among other things it:
- determines which points you'll include,
- determines how much detail to add to those points,
- determines which (if any) visual aids you'll use, and
- measures if you've delivered a great presentation or not.

How can it measure if I've made a great presentation or not?

If you achieved your presentation objective, you have; if you did not, you didn't, (sorry). But before this measurement, your objective is vital for my number one rule in all presentations, IF IT DOESN'T ADD, IT SUBTRACTS.

If what doesn't add, it subtracts?

Everything in your presentation; every single thing. Every word, every gesture, every visual aid, every thought you introduce and point you make: IF IT DOESN'T ADD, IT SUBTRACTS.

Add to what?

Add to helping you achieve your objective. I want you

to be very disciplined on this. If a point or a visual aid or anything in your presentation does not add to helping you achieve your objective, throw it out! We'll use my ADD - SUBTRACT rule ruthlessly in the next few steps but for now, know that it can only be used when you have a valid objective.

But aren't some tangents allowed, if only to give my audience a break?

No. Tangents are not allowed. *Especially* not to give your audience a break. It's hard enough to focus an audience's attention on your points without you providing tempting diversions. When you go merrily skipping down the lane to off-the-tracksville, your audience will follow as surely as Mary's Little Lamb. You're saying in effect, "this will be more fun than what we have been going over, let's play a little bit." The ugly problem occurs when it's time to bring them home to your real presentation. Some audience members never come back (bye-bye) and others resent they must. Tangents stand in the way of you achieving your objective and when it comes to that, you must be as tunnel-visioned as Sunday the Cat.

Sunday the Cat?

We have two cats, Sunday and Monday (don't even ask). If Sunday could speak, she would make a fine presenter because she only thinks about one thing in her little cat brain: achieving her objective. If you put a new, strange item on the floor, Sunday will immediately go over to sniff it.

If you gently push her away from it before she satisfies her curiosity, she'll go right back to it. In fact, if you continue to push her away one hundred times, she'll still try to go right back to it. I've tried this with her on any number of occasions (which shows you what a fascinating life I lead) and her reaction is inevitably the same. Sunday doesn't get mad and she never gives up. She just has her objective in mind and nothing else matters.

Monday, on the other paw, is easily distracted in the same situation. If you call her name after putting the object down, she'll walk over to you expecting a pet. If you put a familiar cat treat down next to the item, she'll eat it and then beg for another, completely forgetting about the object. Monday can be distracted by noises, smells, food, and sometimes Monday is even distracted by things no one but Monday sees or hears. In other words, Monday is much more like a common meandering presenter who is distracted from his objective many times in the course of his presentation.

What distracts most presenters from achieving their objective?

Lots of things. Opening jokes or stories that have little relevance to the objective. Wondering whether audience members can read their visual aids. Noticing that the boss doesn't look too happy that morning. Cramming in a plethora of details and then getting lost in explaining one minor aspect of one minor point. Tough questions from audience members. A lack of rehearsal. Remembering a story in the middle of explaining a point. In other words, just about everything.

Won't these things happen anyway?

Not with a strong, clear objective firmly in mind - and maybe in your pocket. A few years ago, I was coaching the newly formed sales staff of a large chemical company. The sales manager was frustrated because the salespeople seemed to forget their objectives especially in front of customers during sales presentations (a particularly inconvenient time to forget your objective).

If a customer asked a question in the middle of one of

these presentations, some salespeople would immediately abandon their rehearsed talks and focus in on that customer's concern. Although this was sometimes acceptable if there was only one customer in the room, most times, there were many more customers present and few of them cared in the least about that specific point. Worse, if a customer asked a particularly demanding (read: rude) question, some new salespeople hit their "junkyard dog button" and launched a verbal debating assault that demolished their victims' points - and promptly lost them sales.

To counter these unfortunate lapses, I came up with the idea of having each salesperson write his specific objective for a sales call on a 3" by 5" card which he placed in his breast pocket. His presentation and question and answer period then revolved around that card. If what he was about to say or do would help him achieve the card's objective, he would say or do it. If not, he was not to say or do it.

Years later the sales manager told me this one simple idea saved his company countless dollars, a lot of wasted time, and a tremendous amount of unneeded aggravation.

Is it better to have multiple objectives or no objective?

Would you prefer cutting off your arm or your leg? If your choice really gets down to this horrible level, on the day of your presentation, pretend to have a profound religious experience that strikes you mute and just hope for the best.

But I never have just one presentation objective!

Then you're just like a lot of presenters. But audience members don't listen to a lot of presenters because when they can't figure out where a presenter is taking them, they become confused, bored, resentful, and then amnesic (usually in that order).

If you truly have more than one specific objective (and you're just not using this as an excuse for not deciding on one objective) there is something you can do: divide your presentation into a number of smaller presentations; each with its own objective.

If you have two specific objectives and twenty minutes to speak, think of your presentation as two distinct ten-minute units. Each unit would then have its own objective and its own supporting points. A common opening and closing would still be appropriate.

Do I state my objective to my audience?

Yes, in most cases. Although it's not absolutely essential, most audience members like to hear in clear terms what you're trying to achieve with them that day.

Is there ever an objective you don't state to an audience?

Sure. One example is if you're a salesperson who has just been invited to speak to a group "for informational purposes only." You know you cannot explicitly give a sales presentation but you also know that every piece of information you deliver must help you make an eventual sale. Your stated objective is, "To inform my audience about the XYZ;" your real objective is "To convince my audience to buy the XYZ."

But isn't that two objectives?

No. It's one stated objective and one silent objective. And that adds up to one presentation objective for the audience - at least by the way I count. And I'm the only one who's counting in this book.

What if the audience doesn't agree with my objective?

You lose. I always tell my seminar participants, "a presenter and an audience are like an egg and a rock. It doesn't matter if the egg hits the rock or the rock hits the egg. In either case, it's not going to go well for the egg."

You have an objective to achieve with your presentation. You simply cannot achieve that objective if the audience comes in that day expecting to hear something else. It really doesn't matter who was at fault in understanding what was to be presented, if the audience doesn't accept your objective, you can't achieve it.

How can I make sure the audience understands my objective?

Put it in writing. Most presentations have some form of written communication that precedes them. Obviously, you (or someone) must tell audience members where to meet, on which day, and at which time. This communication vehicle might take the form of a memo, a letter, an advertisement, a poster, or even a message on a bulletin board. Whichever form it takes, in addition to the usual information it conveys, it should also clearly state your objective.

If audience members read the necessary information and have a problem with your objective, you'll hear about it.

Next, you should restate your objective somewhere near the beginning of your actual presentation. If audience members then object to it, at least you've covered yourself with a tangible piece of hard copy.

Will all audience members read it?

Are you kidding? Of course not! Most audience members will read it and do what they're supposed to do but there will be some who don't. There will be some who read it and forget it, some who read it and ignore it, and some who selectively read and zip right past your objective. You've done the best you can do by putting it in writing. Although this is not a perfect answer to the problem, it's a whole lot better than wasting an entire presentation on people who expect to hear something else.

What if audience members won't agree to any number of the objectives I submit?

I would question if they're really disagreeing with the objectives or actually disagreeing with what they anticipate you'll say or the very idea of you speaking at all. Agreement between audience members and the presenter on the presentation objective is one of the fundamental prerequisites of this form of communication. If done correctly, it saves everyone a lot of time and effort.

But if I have a "want him to do" objective, isn't he agreeing to do what I want if he accepts the objective?

Not at all. If your audience member accepts a persuasive objective, he's merely allowing you the opportunity to convince him. He's certainly not offering a guarantee he'll be convinced.

Think of television commercials. When we watch a commercial, we know what the sponsor's objective is: he wants us to buy his product. By watching, we give him the opportunity to convince us to buy his product - but that doesn't mean we will buy it.

Why do I write the objective before the opening?

Creating and delivering presentations are two very different things. This seems to confuse many presenters. They think, "if I'm going to say something first, I must write it first." This isn't true. Your objective is the foundation of your presentation. You can't create a building without first laying the foundation. You'd be a strange architect to try to slip in the foundation after completing the walls and roof - and you'd have a strange looking building.

When I hear some strange sounding presentations, I know I'm often listening to talks that are being delivered in the same order in which they were first thought. Please don't let me hear these strange thoughts from you.

Anything else on my objective?

Just one thing. Objectives are like certain extreme poker hands; with them, "you know right away." In other words, you pretty much know the outcome of any poker round if the hand you've just been dealt is a royal straight flush. You're probably going to win. In the same vein, you pretty much know the score if you're dealt cards like I'm usually dealt: cards that bear no actual resemblance to one another. The suits on my cards are always different, the numbers don't match and aren't close together, in fact, I've even been dealt cards from different decks.

The only advantage to being dealt hands like this is "you know right away." If I haven't caught a bad case of the "card hopes" that night, I throw down the ugly hand and stop contributing bucks to my friends' good times.

It's the same with an objective, "you'll know right away." If you can't form a simple, clear, one-sentence objective for your presentation, chances are, it's not going to get any better. Don't waste your time trying to make it work with more details or fancier words or pretty visual aids. There's no presentation technique or trick in the world that will save a presentation from a crummy objective.

Either rethink the objective or rethink the presentation.

Summary

This is the objective step of your presentation and one of the most critical to my formula. Objectives are the foundations of presentations. Virtually everything else is built on top of them. If you don't have a good objective, you won't have a good presentation.

Since most audience members expect to be bored during parts of most dull, meandering presentations, they respond well to presenters who state in a clear, precise manner, "this is what I'll achieve in this presentation." They know these are rare presenters who've taken the time to prepare, have considered their audiences' needs, and have rehearsed.

Do you know there are audiences out there who have never in their lives heard a great presentation with a great objective? Please make sure that's not still true the next time you present.

STEP 3
WHY SHOULD HE DO THIS?
OR WHAT DO YOU WANT
HIM TO KNOW?

If your objective (from Step 2) is the foundation of your presentation, Step 3 is the supporting structure. Easy-to-understand structure is essential for every great presentation from street corner arguments to highly technical lectures. The reason is simple: people can't learn new information in a vacuum. They have to relate unknown ideas to things that they do know or mentally put those ideas in a logical order that makes sense to them. And this is true for both persuasive and informative presentations.

Let's use food shopping for an example. Pretend you and I are going to prepare dinner; you'll do the shopping and I'll do the cooking. If I asked you to pick up eggs, apples, frankfurters, bananas, cabbage, and donuts, you might begin to question my culinary abilities and start thinking of restaurants. But assume I can convince you to go shopping for those items anyway.

Now close your eyes and imagine yourself in the middle of a large supermarket with two of my ten dollar bills in your hand. What were those items I asked you to buy? Don't read the previous paragraph, (you cheat!) When you come trudging back with a package of stale donuts under your arm, and listen to my nagging lecture #9 - "The Wisdom of Shopping Lists," you'll feel as confused and resentful as most audience members after most presentations.

But if I knew that "people don't learn in vacuums, they need an order that makes sense to them" before telling you what I wanted you to buy, we'd do much better. What if I

49

said, "My shopping list is as easy as ABC. A is for apples. B is for bananas. C is for cabbage. D is for donuts. E is for eggs. And F is for frankfurters." Don't you think you'd remember more of the list? Of course you would. We might still go to a restaurant but at least you'd have bought the right stuff.

You remember much more in this example because you've associated unknown information (my grocery list) with a known logical, sequencing order (the alphabet). It's the same in presentations. You can't dump a "dog's breakfast" of disorganized facts in front of audience members and hope they make some sense out of it when you obviously couldn't. Besides, it's not their job to organize it for you. You must organize it, structure it, and put it in a logical order to clearly explain the facts that support your objective.

How many points can I use to support my objective?

As many as you want but research and common sense tell us audiences will only learn a very limited number of points in most presentations. My rule of thumb is to start with two basic points. Others can be added at your own risk. If you have more than four or five points in a persuasive presentation, chances are you'll overwhelm your audience.

Informative presentations may have more than four or five points but certainly no more than nine or ten. If you have more information to deliver, consider dividing your presentation into a number of smaller presentations or try an alternative method of communication.

But my (idea) (product) (company) (life) is much more complicated than that! I NEED to deliver more points!

No point is important if your audience doesn't hear it because they've stopped listening. You're not delivering a presentation to fulfill a need in your life by pouring out your heart and your head. You're delivering a presentation to do one thing: achieve your objective. That's it. IF IT DOESN'T ADD, IT SUBTRACTS. And an unending gush of "important facts" certainly does not add to achieving your objective.

Years ago I worked for an advertising agency and had the dreadful task of writing a print ad for a new centrifugal pump.

The company ad manager was very excited because this new pump had about seventeen fantastic features which would supposedly race the heart of pump lovers everywhere. I took the top three features and created a good, strong professional ad that would stop readers and (perhaps) motivate them to learn more about the product from a brochure or a salesperson. As anyone in advertising will tell you, that's about the most a good print ad can do; no one buys capital equipment based only on the information in an advertisement. At least they don't if they want to stay in business very long.

When the ad manager saw the copy, he frantically called my office. He sounded like he had just been informed his young children were sold to work in Bulgarian coal mines. He said I had emasculated his new pump (a truly boggling concept to me) and where were the other fourteen points? When I calmly explained that readers rarely read ads with seventeen points and we had the research to prove it, he became even more incensed. He demanded that I rewrite the ad with all of his points and even included two more for good measure!

Of course you're probably thinking I gathered my print ad research and the account supervisor, rationally explained the situation to our client, convinced him to run a successful three point ad, and saved him thousands of dollars. Like hell. I wrote the ad just as he told me to write it and, after fifteen years, he's still waiting for it's first call.

What cost that ad manager thousands of dollars to learn, you can learn right now for next to nothing: people neither want nor need countless points to be convinced. If they're the right points, you can convince them in two or three.

But isn't achieving understanding in presentations different than achieving it in print ads?

You bet it is. It's much harder in presentations. When we read for information, two critical learning factors come into play. First, we read at our own speed. If we're fast readers, we read material quickly, if we're slow readers, we read it slowly. Second, if we don't understand something and are motivated to learn it, we'll go back to the material and reread it.

Now consider oral presentations. Here the responsibility for both critical learning factors, speed and the ability to go over the material again, has shifted from the "reader" to the presenter. Now the presenter determines at what speed the information is delivered. And if it wasn't understood initially and he does not repeat it, there's no chance to learn it again.

If you had any difficulty understanding this concept, simply reread the preceding two paragraphs (we'll wait). This is a luxury we have in written communication that we don't have in presentations. That's why presentations must be very simple, very clear, and why points must be repeated.

Why do you make such a big deal about numbering my points?

Audiences can't learn your information in a vacuum. As I've said, they must associate your unknown (to them) ideas with something they do know. Assuming they know how to count, they can then fill in the imaginary blanks next to these numbers with your ideas.

Besides numbers, aren't there other logical structures I can use?

Sure. But unless you have a very good reason to veer off the numbered track, it's best to stick to the numbers. If you want to try something a little different, you may use the "past - present" or "before x - after x" logical sequencing orders since these are already fixed in the minds of audience members. Remember my shopping list? That lent itself to the alphabet because I was able to associate the first letters of the items to the first letters of the alphabet.

Although these are alternative methods of logically sequencing your ideas (and there are others), most presentations should be done "by the numbers."

Why am I still finding it difficult to simplify my presentation down to two or three points?

Possibly because of moral ineptitude, a genetic defect, or a lack of civilized upbringing but probably because you're just not used to doing it this way. Inexperienced presenters remind me of inexperienced writers. New writers use big words in order to impress people but what they usually end up doing is obfuscating their intended assimilators of information (or, as old writers say, confuse the hell out of their readers).

It's the same in presentations. New presenters try to cram in as many points and as much detail as possible to impress audience members with their knowledge and competence. What they end up doing is putting audience members to sleep.

I once coached a woman who had a hard time simplifying everything in her life. She decided she would make no exceptions for presentations and she continued to deliver talks that were so complicated no one could understand them. About this same time, I picked up some new book that said the world was divided into two types of people: simplifiers and complicators. When I explained the theory to her, her reaction was predictable. "Obviously," she groaned, "the theory was conceived by a simplifier!"

Why do people complicate their lives and their presentations? I don't know but I do know that when it comes to presentations, simpler is always better. Always.

If I present in this simple manner, won't audiences think I'm being superficial?

Not at all. Simplicity and superficiality are two very different things. Let's use an example. The objective of your presentation is "to convince my audience to invest in municipal bonds," and your supporting points are "1. low-risk, and 2. relatively high yield." Now you just know this is going to be an in-depth presentation on some complicated financial matters but you also can see it will be pretty easy to follow. It's simple but certainly not superficial.

Why must I limit my points to only two or three words?

Two reasons: 1. so your audience can remember your points easier, and 2. so you can. Now I know this is tough for a lot of people at first but that's because you're not used to doing things this way. It does get easier after you've done it a few times.

The easiest way to limit the words in each of your points is what I call the "Why? Because!" Method:

1. Turn your objective into a question. If you take the example above, your question is, "Why should my audience invest in municipal bonds?"

2. Write your answer out in a complete sentence. The answer is, "Because municipal bonds are low risk investments for the vast majority of investors." (I know your fourth or fifth grade teacher told you not to begin sentences with the word "because" but do it anyway. I won't tell.)

3. Next, start crossing out words until you get down to the two or three that make the most sense, in this case, "low risk."

4. Do this for each point and then put the points in the best order that you can determine. In the example above, it just seems smarter to talk about risk before talking about yield. Obviously I know very little about financial matters but this order "feels" right to me.

I can see why this simplified structure helps my audience remember my points, but how can it help me?

Because it frees you from notes. A well-structured, well-rehearsed presentation can usually be delivered without notes and this impresses audience members far more than it should. We'll learn much more about your delivery in Chapter 9 but for now, know that this simplified structure frees you in ways you probably don't even know exist.

If a presenter doesn't have to try to remember a multitude of information and a jumble of barely related facts in his presentation, he's free to focus on powerful aspects of oral communication. He can command the audience's attention with brilliant eye contact. He can please the audience's ears with impressive vocal variance and dramatic pauses. He can do all sorts of things - once he's freed from trying to remember what to say next. And he can help free himself by using only two or three points, each limited to only two or three words.

One evening while attending a concert, I was moved by a compelling piano piece played by an obviously gifted musician. After a few moments of enjoyment I realized the lyric was the same tune my neighbor's six-year old daughter banged out always to my great annoyance. I was shocked! How could the same piece be so absolutely different?

Then I realized the difference. The concert pianist long ago learned the notes and the movement of the piece. It was only after this that he was able to add the feeling and depth that made the tune magical.

It's the same in presentations. If you're ever to be a great presenter, learning the points and structure "cold" is only the beginning. Certainly well over ninety per cent of all presentations never even get this far! But it will be only after you know your "notes" that you can add the feeling and depth to make your presentation memorable.

Is there another advantage to using just a few points each with a few words?

Yes, but I'm a little uncomfortable expressing it because of what it implies. Here it is: people are often lazy thinkers, lazy listeners, and lazy communicators. They sometimes do all of these things in mindless cliches and dubious "group thought." So if a good presenter builds a strong rapport with audience members; that is, if they like, trust, and respect him as a presenter, they often have a tendency to let him think and communicate for them.

Take the "buy the XYZ telecommunications system" example. If that was delivered by a good presenter in a dynamic way and audience members trusted the presenter, chances are they would remember and accept the two-word, two point supporting structure (1. cost effectiveness and 2. lifetime guarantee) without extensive thought and analysis. If someone else then asks them about the system, chances are they would parrot back those points because they're so simple and easy to understand.

The problem arises, of course, with presenters who have "questionable" ethics. What is an acceptable and elegant presentation structure with its roots in simplicity may then become a clever, manipulative tool with its roots in dishonesty. The structure itself is effective and amoral; it's the good presenter who decides if it will be used in a moral or immoral manner.

The advantage in this structure capitalizes on peoples' love of simple understanding without thinking too hard. The disadvantage arises when the technique falls into the wrong hands. Countless politicians, car salespeople, and former spouses can testify to its effectiveness.

Summary

People can't learn information in a vacuum, they need a logical sequential order that makes sense to them to understand your points. That's why it's especially critical to limit your points, limit the words in each point, and number the points.

To begin, I suggest two strong points for persuasive presentations ("want him to do" presentations) and only two or three words in each point. You may expand on this, but in most cases, I don't believe it will help you. If you have the right two or three points that's usually enough to convince an audience of most reasonable objectives. In informative presentations ("want him to know" presentations) more points are allowed but certainly not an unlimited number.

Simplicity and structure are the most essential written elements of any presentation. Regardless of how technical or how much detail you later include, you must start with an understandable structure. Since many people find it difficult at first to be this disciplined, I will include a list of examples on the next few pages to demonstrate what I'm talking about and how easy it is to do once you get the hang of it.

By the way, you should know, the loudest groans I get from my seminar participants are the ones I hear when I ask them to support their objectives in only two points, each limited to two or three words. There's usually much wailing and gnashing of teeth and moaning of "that's impossible," "can't do that!" "we don't do it that way," etc. When I demand that they stop sniveling and get on with the assignment, you would be amazed at how quickly they take to it.

Before the day is out, they've stopped cursing me and often burst into song on the virtues of presentation structure.

I'm quite sure if some were involved in domestic disputes after the seminar, they would say, "Darling, I think you're being unreasonable for two basic reasons, number one, you're tired and number two, you're overworked." (I hope their success rate on this approach is better than mine.)

Examples of Objectives and Supporting Points

PERSUASIVE PRESENTATIONS: (Ask Yourself "WHY?")

Objective:
To convince my audience to buy the XYZ telecommunications system. (WHY?)
Points:
1. Cost - effective, and
2. Lifetime guarantee.

Objective:
To convince my audience to vote for Candidate X.
Points:
1. His experience, and
2. His vision.

Objective:
To convince my audience to exercise 30 minutes a day.
Points:
1. Better health, and 2. Better looks.

Objective:
To convince my audience to give to the United Way.
Points:
1. Helps community, and
2. Helps you (tax deduction).

Objective:
To convince my audience to attend a function.
Points:
1.   Help cause, and
2. Good time.

Objective:
To convince my audience to buy more copies of this book.
Points:
1.Great gifts, and
2. Help author.

INFORMATIVE PRESENTATIONS: (ASK YOURSELF "WHAT?")

Objective:
To tell my audience the most important elements of my job. (WHAT?)
Points:
1. Managing people, and
2. Managing time.

Objective:
To tell my audience the most important things to learn in this class.
Points:
1. Who,
2. When, and
3. Why.

Objective:
To tell my audience what to look for in a diamond.
Points:
1. Carat,
2. Clarity,
3. Cut, and
4. Cost.

STEP 4
CREATE "ACTIVE"
VISUAL AIDS

If you've ever attended one of my lectures or seminars, you probably learned in about the first five minutes how I feel about visual aids. I dislike them. More accurately, I dislike what they've become. Like television advertising commercials, what started out as a good idea has turned into an unmanageable and annoying distraction.

Today's visual aids dehumanize presentations. They function as electronic excuses for mediocre presenters. They gobble up dollars which should be used for training actual human beings to communicate with other human beings. They act as notes, as barriers, and as flashy indicators of the amount of money some people are willing to invest in jaded audiences. Worse, they've become the focal points of many presentations. Presenters, once proud human beings with noble ideas and the ability to eloquently express them, are reduced to being the "schleppers for the slides."

Corporations, in a transparency attempt to slide over the inadequacies of poorly trained presenters, standardize their presentations with glitzy visuals that can be shown by anyone. Indeed, if an employee scheduled to present that day is squashed like a bug by a bus, his fortunate coworker on the curb could pick from the street his briefcase of visuals and deliver virtually the exact presentation to the client.

Some pathetic presenters even begin their talks with a visual announcing their names! Since we must assume the poor mopes could once speak their own names and introduce themselves like civilized human beings, we must now conclude they feel compelled to include this vital information in transparencies or slides for electronic credibility or because they fear their minds will turn to mush if they face audience members without their "cable crutches."

Now, at the risk of sounding wishy-washy on the subject of visual aids, I will state that they have their place if used properly. However, if they're used commonly, they hurt many more presentations than they aid.

Visual aids are just that: "aids." They are not presentations themselves. They are not even the focal point of presentations. They cannot save a dull presentation nor rescue a mediocre presenter. When you add "pretty pictures" to dumb presentations, they just become expensive dumb presentations. When you put before an audience an incomprehensible deluge of dull information that resembles a blueprint for a nuclear reactor, turn down the lights, and speak in a monotone, you're inviting the audience to nap. And forget about pointers and laser pointers to focus attention on what you want people to read. People read what they want to read when they want to read it; they've been doing it for years.

Equally ineffective is the "transparency strip tease" as presenters alternately cover and then slowly reveal that part of the picture they want the audience to read. I've literally heard audience members yell, "take it off!" during these follies! They were not referring to the clothes of the presenter.

Visual aids form one area where great presenters must go back to the original concept of the idea and start with a clean slate. When they use their minds and imagination, they often come to the conclusion that for most audiences, "active" or "note-taking" visual aids are far superior than anything that has to be plugged into a wall.

But how do you REALLY feel about visual aids?

I hate to be ambiguous on the subject, so let me tell you a few *other* things I don't like about them:

Wretched Repairs: A rule I give to seminar participants is, "If you can't fix it fast, don't bring it.   When a bulb blows, 'the guy who does A-V' - is usually home watching TV."

Have you ever watched a nervous presenter trying to change a hot slide projector bulb that has just blown? The visual (and audio) excitement usually exceeds anything that has appeared on the screen.

"Who Knows How to Run This Thing?" Do you ever notice the looks on the faces of presenters who confidently push a button on a video or overhead projector and nothing happens?   Their eyes become wider as they push the button again and again and then give it a real jolt. Within seconds they've hit every button on the machine all the while peppering the audience with half-witty one liners like, "Gosh, this worked before!" or "What am I doing wrong here?"

Quick Clickers. I call nervous presenters who "click" (advance or reverse) their own slides "quick clickers." I also call them crazy. Inevitably their anxiety finds its way to their fingers and soon they're talking about something that was on the screen about six slides ago. Seeing the puzzled looks of audience members, they quickly see they're lost, announce that fact to an audience which already knows, and madly start clicking in reverse. These blurring light shows have been known to give former hippies hallucinogenic flashbacks.

People Who Talk About Their Aids. Much of the mindless chatter which I refer to as "presentation pollution" stems from talk about visual aids. Besides taking away from the performance aspect of presentations (can you imagine an actor talking about the cost of a set?) this babble is a complete waste of the audience's time. Promise me you will never utter anything close to: "Hope you like these slides; they cost us fifty bucks each." or "I think this is the transparency that goes here. I just picked these up from our agency this morning." or "These overheads are from a talk I gave a few weeks ago but I think you'll get the idea." (In other words, "Of course you're not important enough to create new visuals; I hope you don't mind leftovers.")

O.K. but what if my boss requires us to use visual aids?

It seems you have four choices: eliminate your boss, eliminate your job, use visual aids like everyone else, or use your head. If you use your head, here are my suggestions:

1. Make sure your boss demands visual aids. Did he or she say you must or have you assumed this is true because everyone has always done it this way? Does it make sense for you to spend the time and money for fancy visual aids? Will they really enhance your presentation? Appeal to your boss's sense of good business.
2. Make sure you're required to use the visual aids that you're now using. "Active" or "Note-taking" visual aids from Step 4 are visual aids. In fact, they're often better than what we commonly think of as visual aids because they require audience members to take a more dynamic role in your presentation. They're also cheaper and easier to create.
3. If it makes sense (or you absolutely must) go "electronic," here's the best way to do it: The Room Light Open/Room Light Close.

This is absolutely the most important piece of advice I can ever give you on electronic visual aids. Remember - your presentation begins before the lights go and it ends after the lights are up. Take at least two or three minutes before you start the visual aid show to establish a rapport with your audience with the lights on.

Include in this "room light open:" your strong opening

(covered in Step 6) and your preview (see Preview-Go Through-Review, page 114). Do not use notes unless you must. Establish commanding eye contact. You must make a significant, clear impression on audience members here because they'll only hear your voice in a few minutes. If it's possible, memorize these first few minutes (one of the few times I would ever suggest this drastic step) so you'll be free to do everything you can to make a compelling opening impression.

When the visuals are done, have the room lights turned back on, establish yourself before the audience again in the same commanding way, quickly review what they've just seen and present your closing in as forceful a manner as you think reasonable.

This is the only way a great presenter would ever use electronic visual aids because he knows he must command the audience's attention away from the "glitzier" - but less effective - focal point. The most effective communication in the world is between individual human beings. Electronic "enhancers" can help the message but they will never become the sole communicators in great presentations.

What else do I need to know about electronic visual aids?

Here are a few "quickies:"

• the best visuals express very simple concepts, key words, bulletted points, simple graphics - but not together. Details are for handouts.

• your first slide or transparency is for focus only. Don't focus in and out on the important points of your presentation; this just makes them look less important. Ideally, you will have everything in focus and the projectors off before audience members arrive.

• if you say "Can everyone see this?" you might as well also wear a sign that says "Presenter Trainee." Good presenters check their visual aids from every seat in the house long before audience members arrive.

• never speak when you are changing transparencies. Better yet, have someone else change them for you. While you are "standing next to the screen, not next to the machine," (another rule of mine) simply give a prearranged signal to the "changer." If you must change overheads yourself, rehearse enough to do it well! And don't speak into that whirring machine! Save your voice for the audience.

What about "write-along" visual aids like chalk boards?

They're fine - if you don't mind audience members writing you off. The average presenter speaks about 150 words per minute. The average audience can easily think four or five times faster than that. How many words can you legibly write per minute? Fifteen? Twenty? As you're plodding along like Miss Frances from "Ding Dong School," your audience is thinking ten times faster than that. One suspects they are not thinking of you.

How long should the same aid be on the screen?

There's no definite rule here. The correct purpose of visual aids is to augment verbal presentations. If they were meant to act as "stand alone" pieces, they'd have to be changed continuously to keep an audience's attention. But to structure an audience's attention or to help visually explain a concept which would be more difficult to explain without a "picture," the aid should be on the screen as long as it takes to do its job.

Besides your "active" visual aids, are there any others you like?

Sure. First off, my active aids (like the one on page 7) make wonderful screen images if they can't be copied and passed out (of course they're no longer considered "active" if they're just on the screen). They augment the verbal presentation. They aren't the "show" themselves; the audience must listen to the presenter for that - but they structure the audience's thinking and help them see a point's relationship to the objective.

I also like visual aids with simple questions on them that force audience members to listen to presenters for answers. This is as it should be: the aids are the supporting actors; the presenter is the star.

As a matter of fact, I do like visual aids for what they originally were and what they can be used for. I just don't like what they've been generally accepted to be in today's presentations: necessary excuses and crutches for mediocre presenters.

Anything else on visual aids?

Three quick things. First, don't talk to your aids; they should have heard your presentation before. It's terribly distracting to audience members when an inexperienced presenter turns his back to them and starts speaking to images on the screen or the wall. Many times they can't hear him which is just as well because what he's usually doing is using his aids as notes. Visual aids are not notes. They are not there to help you; they're there to help your audience members. Get your own notes! Better yet, learn the major points of your presentation so well you don't need notes.

Second, never apologize to an audience for your visual aids. If they're crummy - don't show them! If they're the best you've got, and you need them, treat them like the most professionally produced pieces of commercial art in the world. I once saw an electrical engineer from a major company hold up a piece of a paper bag on which he first conceived an original, brilliant electrical system design. The bag had grease stains and scribble scratches on it but the audience didn't even notice. They saw the fire in the engineer's eyes and the reverential way he handled his sketch and all of a sudden it seemed like one of the most important pieces of paper in the world. It was also, truly, a visual aid. The man could not have told his story as well without it.

Finally, when thinking about visual aids, think of Lincoln's Gettysburg address. Can you think of one transparency that would have aided that talk? How about an opening joke? Great communication does not need more gimmicks - it needs more of you presenting at your best.

Summary

"Active" visual aids are those in which the audience participates, usually in the form of note taking. These are the aids I suggest in Step 4. The wisdom of using most other visual aids, especially the electronic enhancers or overhead and slide projectors, should be examined very carefully.

When used correctly, visual aids can augment an oral presentation. When used commonly, they act as a barrier between presenters and their audiences. What usually happens is that visual aids take on far more significance than they should and the presenter becomes merely an "aid to the aid." Visual aids are often misused as an excuse for mediocre presenters and presentations. In fact, the very best visual aids can do is enhance human communication - they can never replace it.

What About Microphones?

Since we're in the neighborhood and just finished visiting visual aids, we probably should stop in and pay a friendly visit to audio aids. Welcome to the wonderful world of microphones. Audio aids are only distant relatives to visual aids. Some might even call them crazy aunts best kept locked in the attic. When microphones behave, they can enhance a presentation to an audience of more than a large roomful of people.

But microphones rarely behave near the mouths of inexperienced presenters. They squeal. They screech. They teasingly fade in and out. They pop "p's" and hiss "s's." They pick up all kinds of radio signals and sounds and sometimes they even play dead. They don't like to hang around amplifiers or water and many seem to have electrical cords that are more frayed than Don King's hair.

They're not especially fond of new presenters. A nervous speaker who merely rattles his pocket change when he doesn't use a microphone decides to use one and suddenly sounds like he's kicking snow tire chains around the stage. Mikes like to both surprise and shock beginning presenters. They surprise them with inhuman shrieks or dead air and audiences inevitably blame the presenter for audio belches and gaps in sound.

Microphones shock speakers too - literally. There's nothing quite like the sound of an anxious presenter as he firmly grasps a "hot" microphone and bellows his agony into the electronic enhancer only inches from his mouth. It's really kind of tough to turn a presentation around after an opener like that.

But what microphones do to presenters pales in comparison to what presenters do to them! Probably the most common (and least awful) thing presenters do to microphones is turn them off. I've seen numerous presenters walk up to perfectly good mikes they know were working just a few seconds before and, without thinking, turn them right off.

Of course some witty dialogue usually follows with the speaker mouthing the words "Is this thing on?" like Marcel Marceau without greasepaint and some loud audience volunteers shouting for him to turn it on while others shake their heads in answer to his unheard question.

Other presenters knock mikes over, drop them, inadvertently spit into them, and yank their heads off while trying to adjust them. Other people on the program immediately jump into the fracas. The audience members get a few chuckles as they watch techidiots who look more like the Three Stooges than anyone they'd want to hear present that day.

It's all a lot of fun unless you're serious about establishing audience credibility and communicating a dynamic message. Now from reading any of the other pages in this book, I'm sure you know I'm neither against humor nor fun in presentations. I'm just against it at your expense and if it costs you audience credibility.

I have just two rules regarding microphones. Both are very simple. The first is: don't use a microphone, unless you must. The second? If you must, don't use it for the first time in front of your audience.

It would be silly to try to speak to a room of 300 people without a microphone unless you're a professional speaker with an outstanding, trained voice. It's equally foolish to speak to a small group of people for which you don't really need a microphone even if one is provided. Too many inexperienced presenters fall into the "if it's there, I guess I'm supposed to use it" trap.

The simple reason for not using microphones unless you really need them is there are just too many things that can go wrong. Now there are cases on record of inexperienced presenters walking up to untested mikes and completely going through their presentations without problems. I think the last one was in Wisconsin in 1957. Using a microphone well takes knowledge, practice, and experience. There aren't many short cuts.

There are other good reasons not to use microphones unless you absolutely must. One is called projection. In Chapter 9 when we talk more about your voice and what it can do, you'll learn that proper projection is vital for a great presentation. Please understand that projection is not volume. Among other things, presentation projection involves vocal variance (the "punches" and "pauses" of your speech), enthusiasm, and commitment.

Volume only involves loudness. Microphones only control volume. If you take a dull presenter with a dreary, monotonic voice and put him in front of a microphone, all you've done is turned up the volume on his dullness. As dumb as this sounds, there are many people who believe that somehow microphones can transform a blah voice into an exciting one. I wish it were that easy!

I always tell beginning speakers to stand away from the microphone and project in their normal presentation voice. Of course this flies in the face of what they are usually told by meeting planners and others who seem to know what they're talking about in this area.

Who's right? Decide for yourself. As you practice my second microphone rule, (coming up) try a simple experiment. While someone who knows your presentation objective is listening in the middle of the room, give your opening with your lips inches away from the mike. You won't have to speak too loudly to be heard. Next, stand about a foot and a half away from the mike and deliver the same opening in your regular, presentation projection. Ask your listener which sounds better If he agrees with me, believe him.

My second microphone rule is: if you must use a microphone, don't use it for the first time in front of your audience. Let me be very specific here. I'm not talking about rehearsing with just any old microphone before you're scheduled to present; I'm talking about rehearsing with the same, exact microphone you'll be using with your audience.

To me, microphones seem to have as many different personalities as people. Two of them just never seem to react the same way in the same situation even if they're exactly alike. So if you must use a microphone, please plan to use the same one before your audience arrives. Usually, arrangements can be made with meeting planners, audio-video technicians, or maintenance people to schedule these vital re-hearsals. And don't be afraid to ask! You have the respon-sibility for the success of the presentation on your shoulders. If people want you to do a good, professional job, they'll help you make the necessary accommodations.

A few quick hints:

• Although lavalier or "lapel" microphones can be trickier than regular, stand up mikes, they allow you greater freedom of movement. While rehearsing with "your" lavalier mike (remember rule 2), it's a good idea to mark the "squeal" areas (where you stand too close to speakers and hear an ugly, electronic shriek) with masking tape on the floor.

• Even though the advertisements "speak very highly of them," wireless mikes still have and cause a lot of problems. Make sure you have a good backup system and the right, new batteries.

Audio aids are like visual aids. If they're used properly, they can enhance your presentations. But if they're used commonly, (that is, like most people use them) they're of-ten more trouble and less interesting than they're worth.

STEP 5
EXPLAIN YOUR POINTS

It happened again just last week. Colleagues of some marketing research people I had coached in one of my seminars came to their own seminar with some exciting feedback from the first group. I had spent the better part of a day in that first seminar trying to convince the researchers to simplify their presentations. They fought me every word of the way.

"You don't know our business," they whined, "people expect all of this detail and explanations of our methodology. They sit there for an hour and read all of our numbers and then question our methods. That's the way it's done!"

"Nonsense!" I sensitively said, "I'll bet your audiences are bored out of their minds! They only want to hear the conclusions and very brief explanations of how you arrived at them. They assume you know what you're doing - that's why they hired you! You don't have to justify your existence in every report to a client."

As I said, this went on in various forms all day long. When I suggested they give their conclusions first and cut their presentations by half if not by two-thirds, they visibly swooned. It was as if I asked them to give up their first born children.

"Deliver three months of work in a half hour presentation? Are you nuts?" they cried, "that's three months of our lives; three months of working day and night! And why should we deliver the conclusions first? We worked three months for the results - surely the client can wait 45 minutes!"

"Why should the client have to wait a minute for the results from research for which he's already paid?" I diplomatically sneered, pouring gasoline on the fire, "He's paying for a simple service - not a part of your lives!"And so it went. The eternal fight over "how much detail?" by the complicators and the simplifier.

Although a lot of the bickering was done in good fun, there was a note of underlying seriousness to the issue. I realized I was dealing with much more than the matter of presentations there. I was questioning how these people made their way in the world. And so of course I treated their point of view with all the respect it deserved.

"Look, complicators" I finally said in exasperation, "I'm not arguing with you any longer. I'm a professional presenter and I've just explained to you for the fourteenth time today why your presentations should be shorter, more structured, and have fewer details. You may follow my advice or you may not. It doesn't matter in the least to me; I get paid the same in either case. Two hours from now, I'll be on a plane heading for my home. You're the ones who are stuck here with a presentation assignment and a few hours of dull details. Do what you want with them."

It was a long ride to the airport. Besides the assignment and the details, I knew the researchers were stuck with something else I had forgotten to mention, a simplifier boss who had hired me in the first place because he received so many client complaints about needlessly long, dull presentations.

He gently made his presence felt by ordering them to state their conclusions first, briefly explain their methodology, and conclude their presentation in less than a half hour. When the client presentation ended, the president of the company thanked the presenters for "the best research presentation I've heard in ten years." Frank Paolo got paid the same, just as he knew he would.

I don't believe your story.

Spoken like a true complicator. But that's O.K. - I get paid the same if you believe it or not. Seriously, variations of that same story have happened to me many times over the last fifteen or twenty years. Although this was a pretty ornery group, they were professional enough to try what their boss asked and were happy to accept the successful results - even if it meant changing the way they did things. No one can ask for more than that.

But how did you know their audience wanted simpler talks?

Their boss told me. He told them too but this sort of "truth" always sounds better from a high-priced consultant they don't see around the office everyday. I don't know why it is, but things always sound better when they're spoken by someone who flies in for the day.

Take motivational speakers. If you read a transcript of some famous aging jock's motivational message that had the salespeople on their feet in utter delirium, you'd find it pretty much comes down to "play hard, play fair, play to win, and be the best you can be." This is probably much the same message your second-grade teacher gave you for free - somehow it just sounds better by a paid presenter.

Anyway, I knew their audience would want a simpler, more structured talk because audiences (almost) ALWAYS want simpler, easy-to-understand talks. I have to include the "almost" because someone, somewhere will remember an audience that wanted more details - at least that's the way the presenter remembers it. I don't trust presenter's memories, however. Nor do I trust completely honest expression by audience members.

What do you mean?

In the rare instances they occur, calls for 'more details' by audience members may mean a lot of things other than 'more details.' Sometimes it means that an audience member doesn't understand a conclusion and wants more of an explanation of how it came to be. Sometimes an audience member disagrees with a conclusion and wants 'more details' to protest the result. Sometimes an audience member calls for 'more details' to show his boss how thorough he is. In any case, most audiences, most times, want fewer rather than more details.

I never hear that.

Of course you don't. Who's going to stand up and criticize you for a "too thorough" job? Who's going to stand up and admit that they stopped listening 45-minutes ago? Like college research papers that are "weighed rather than read," sometimes presentations are judged by their "weight in details" rather than their clear objectives and supporting points based on solid documentation and perceptive insights.

If my audience member is happy with an "information dump," shouldn't I be happy to give it to him?

Certainly not. I doubt if audience members are ever happy with "information dumps." I doubt if most audience members even hear most of them. The fact that they don't stand up and loudly complain probably has more to do with their manners and what they expect from presentations rather than their state of contentment.

But how will I know if I give audiences enough detail?

Here's a fact you'll find hard to accept: you'll never know. There's no magic formula to determine precisely how much information each audience member needs to make a decision. And that's another troubling issue for presenters: each audience member needs a different amount of detail to make a determination. So you will never be able to tell exactlv how much detail is needed and you will never please everyone regardless of how much you include or don't include. Pretty bleak, heh?

So what am I supposed to do?

If you disliked my cold analysis of details and audience members, you'll like my solution even less: err on the side of too few details rather than too many.

What?!

I told you you'd find that one tough, didn't I?

As I stated in Step 5 of Section I, "if you present too little information in an exciting way, audience members will usually ask you for more in a Question and Answer period; but if you present too much information, they'll stop listening, look forward to the end of your presentation and will be reluctant to ask questions for fear of being bored to death again!"

This sentence was worth rereading because convincing presenters to cut details from presentations is one of the toughest jobs I have to do. They cling to their precious little details as if they were strands of life itself. When asked to go through someone's written presentation, I'll arm myself with a red flow pen, my famous "IF IT DOESN'T ADD, IT SUBTRACTS" rule, and start slashing like a drunken pirate. Howls can be heard with each cut.

"Oh, not that!"

"That too?"

"But he's real interested in that point!"

"My boss told me to put that in!"

"My wife told me to put that in !"

"We had this in the last time!"

"Not my color chart!"

"Not my name slide!"

"Not my_____!"

I show no mercy and take no prisoners. When finished, the trembling presenter and I have a lean, mean presentation with severe structure, a single logical objective, a very small number of rational two-word points, and an appointment with presentation destiny. We've given our representative audience member only as much information as we think he needs to achieve our objective. If he'd like more, all he has to do is ask. We'll be prepared. And the whole thing will probably take less than half of the time allotted.

I don't think I like this.

Of course you don't. Most presenters feel secure with a lot of details. They think they have to cover everything and more details is the way to do it. They want to show audiences how smart they are, how much work they've done, how thoroughly they've done the assignment. Audience members pretend they're listening (a skill they learned when they were exposed to their first formal "presenters" - first grade teachers) but in all probability their minds are millions of miles away; just like yours is when you hear most presenters!

There's a lot of research to show that most audience members forget most of what most presenters deliver; usually in a matter of minutes. The problem is they forget the important stuff along with the unimportant stuff. And the reason they can't (or won't take the time to) discover the important stuff is because it's usually buried in a pile of unimportant stuff. IF IT DOESN'T ADD IT SUBTRACTS.

But my work is very technical;
I MUST deliver my details!

Go ahead - but make sure it's to someone who needs (or wants) to hear them. Other techies may wish to listen or maybe your coworkers do but most people probably don't need to become as involved in the subject as you are. That's why the person who knows the most about any subject is usually the person who is the least desirable to speak on it.

Why's that? We always let the person who knows the most about the subject speak about it.

And I can imagine what those presentations sound like. In fact, I don't have to imagine; I hear hundreds of them every year. Let me guess, "too long, very involved, over-the-heads of some audience members, but the guy sure knew his stuff," right? I think I was there - about a million times. Now if you want to give the "expert" some credit, give him a testimonial dinner; better yet, give him a raise, but don't inflict too much of his knowledge on audience members. They don't need to hear it.

Let's take as an example you buying a video camcorder (you've certainly stepped up from shopping for groceries a few chapters ago). You're the "audience" and the salesperson is the "presenter." This salesperson, by the way, is an expert on camcorders. He owns a couple, has taken courses on them, and is even tinkering with a new lens system for one of them. He loves to talk about camcorders. In fact, he loves to talk about them more than sell them.

Into the store you come. The salesperson's eyes light up when you glance at the camcorder case. The sales manager quickly sizes up the scene and pushes the salesman into the stockroom and locks the door.

He walks up to you, takes the cigar out of his mouth, and says, "three things ya gotta know 'bout buying dese cameras: 1. cost—innudderwords—what can you afford? 2. convenience—whadaya want on 'em an' how easy are dey to use? 3. quality—how long will the damn thing last? Now you can see the price tags on 'em for cost. Each of 'em has a brochure right here that tells ya all the gadgets they have. And here's a copy of dat Consumer Reports tellin' ya quality. I'll be by the cash register when yer ready to buy one. Oh, ignore da pounding from dat room—we get some pretty big squirrels around here."

In the same time it would have taken the first salesman to begin to explain "low light lux" to you, the sales manager has zeroed in on your needs, given you a brief amount of structured information, and given you sources for additional information if you need it.

Now class, the question is which salesperson sells more camcorders (or, in presentation terms, is more likely on more occasions to achieve his objective)? The question is not: who knows more about camcorders? Nor is it: with whom would you like to spend more time? There can only be one question in presentations: what's the best way to achieve the objective?

Why is the sales manager selling many more camcorders? Because he's delivering his pitch based on what his "audience" probably wants to hear, not on what he wants to tell them. He probably knows as much about camcorders as he does about stoves and he could probably sell both equally well. His expertise is not in camcorders, it's in "audiences." If the "audience" wants more details, he has an abundance of printed resources at his fingertips written by real experts.

You may not be selling camcorders but in presentations you are "selling" ideas or asking the audience to do something. If you think a "detail dump" is going to help you, well . . . lots of lux.

You like 'stating conclusions first' in presentations. Why?

I'd much rather have audience members listen to my presentation even if they disagree with my conclusions than have them tune out of the presentation, wake up at the conclusions and then find they disagree with me. In the first instance, they'll probably be actively listening to my talk "to see where I went wrong." In the second, they'll know they disagree but don't know why. If they then want to question me, we'll probably have to go over a lot of information other audience members have already heard.

Although you can probably think of exceptions, for most oral presentations, stating conclusions first and then the analysis is a better choice.

I don't have a lot of details in my presentations but I do have extensive analysis. Isn't that different?

It's all pretty much the same if no one is listening. Today, people want good information quickly. Think of CNN News Headlines or 10-second television commercials. The society is moving faster and faster. As presenters, we no longer have the luxury of long discourses or slow, thoughtful discussions. Give audiences only enough information to achieve your objective. They'll appreciate it.

I've cut a lot but I still have a lot of details. Now what?

Consider delivering them in a different form. Spoken presentations are best for concepts, ideas, and moving people. Written presentations are best for extensive analysis, details, and moving information. Why not explain concepts orally and distribute details in written form after you've explained them? The only things that should be passed out during your presentation is the "active" visual aid I talk about in Step 4.

Summary

If it doesn't add, it subtracts.

STEP 6
CHOOSE YOUR OPENING.

Let me ask you a question: what's the worst time for you in a presentation? If you're like most people, the worst time is the minute or two before you actually speak and the first few minutes of your talk. (We'll learn why this is so in Chapter 8 — Stop Worrying.)

Now, let me ask you a second question: when do you think your audience is making its most critical evaluation of you? That's right, those first few seconds of your presentation. So while you're at your worst in terms of presentation anxiety, the audience is making a crucial value judgment of you and your abilities - and we all know how difficult it is to change first impressions. Although this is harsh reality for most people - it will no longer be for you.

Great presenters take advantage of this fact more than any other single element in presentations. Their visual aids may look like others', they may still need notes and some rehearsal on microphones, and their points may not be as clear as they should be, but most know enough to immediately kick off their talks with some drama - some flair. They know that it's far easier to initially impress audience members with a dramatic opening than to try to win them back after a dull start.

First of all, audiences expect very little in the first minutes of any presentation. They're absolutely used to mediocrity. "Good morning, ladies and gentlemen," vanilla speakers drone, "my name is_____ and I'm here to talk about_____." Some gush "what an honor, blah, blah." But my least favorite are the jokers - for them I usually have to squirm in my seat and look at my feet.

Years ago I coached an executive who was to be the M.C. at a large testimonial dinner. I was invited to the dinner (probably in lieu of payment) and took my seat near the head table.

I had written a powerful opening and had coached the speaker thoroughly on the best way to deliver it. Somewhere between our last session and the dinner, he found an old speaker's joke book. He should have found an excuse not to show up that night.

"Good evening, ladies and gentlemen - heh, heh, - oh, I blew it already. My speech coach told me not to start out that way but I guess it's just habit - heh, heh. (Loud squeal from the microphone.) Wow - he also told me not to stand so close to the mike, heh, heh. He was right!" (Titters from the audience.)

Of course by this time I was squirming, looking at my feet, and frantically hoping no one knew that I was the one who did such a bang up job on his coaching. He began again,

"Frank Paolo, sitting right over there, is the one who coached me, so any mistakes I make tonight you can blame on him, heh - heh. Anyway, he also told me not to tell any opening jokes, but I just heard one story recently that reminded me so much of tonight, I think I'll tell it to you anyway, heh - heh.

When I was asked to do so many duties as your host tonight, I was reminded of the eunuch in the King's court. There was just so much to do, he didn't know where to begin. Heh -heh. Neither do I!"

I should have lunged across the head table and brained him on the spot! But I wanly smiled through 45-minutes of mediocrity spiced with idiocy, promising myself I would put his name on every junk mail coupon and religious tract request I could find for a year.

Why was I so upset, you may ask? After all, that was a pretty typical beginning for an after dinner speech; you've probably heard many like it before. It wasn't that bad, was it?

I was angry for two reasons. First, he associated my name and methods with presentation mediocrity. That is an unqualified horror to me. Second, I thought I had inspired him to rise above the rubble, to deliver a powerful and meaningful testimonial that would be a memorable tribute to an honorable man. Obviously, I had not.

Every speaker or potential speaker reading this book right now has a choice: you can rise above that great, gray morass of dull presenters and flat presentations and truly become "distinctively different in a professional way" or you can choose not to. You can choose to communicate with authority, energy, and clarity or you can choose to be a bore. You can choose to move and inspire people, or choose to be a warm visual aid that dumps information.

If you're ever to become a great presenter, you must learn the importance of great openings. The short "formula" opening you learned on page 10 was better than "good morning, ladies and gentlemen," but it's far from a great opening (hey, what do you want in 10-minutes?) A strong presentation opening has three objectives.

1.   A strong opening immediately involves your audience in your subject matter.

I coached the research director of a large corporation who had to speak at a board of directors meeting. He wanted to initiate a new cost-saving procedure that had a hefty, up-front investment. After his introduction, he stood up, walked to the head of the table and said,

"In the time it took me to walk from that seat (pointing to his chair) to this position before you, our company spent over $2000 on research and development. Over 500 of those dollars were wasted. In the next ten minutes I'm going to give you three significant ways we can stop that waste."

Do you think any of the directors thought to themselves, "Gee, he didn't wish me a good morning?" Of course not! They were immediately involved in the presentation and were anxious to hear the rest of it.

Don't waste your audience's time! You don't need more time to make your points, you need to cut the crap, use your mind, and immediately excite their sensibilities with your logic and ideas. If every single word out of your mouth is valuable - especially in the opening minutes - your audience is going to be impressed.

Some speakers tell me they need to "warm up" before they really "get going." Well warm up on your own time! Audience attention is often highest in the opening seconds of your presentation. Don't babble those precious moments away with forced banality, mindless chatter, or dead comic's jokes.

2. A strong opening immediately distinguishes you from most presenters.

Let's face it, most presenters are boring. Worse, audience members expect to be bored at least part of the time in most presentations. When I read that bit of research many years ago, I was shocked. I thought it was me! I thought I was one of the few people in the world who was bored to death by most peoples' speeches. Other audience members seemed to enjoy presentations. Their eyes were open, they appeared to be listening, they clapped and congratulated the presenter at the end. Who knew that many of them were probably just as bored as I was?

Although boredom seems to be accepted by audience members, the ramifications are significant. Think of your thoughts and feelings when you're bored: a lack of concentration, daydreaming, frustration, resentment, sometimes anger. Don't you think these attributes have a considerable effect on how an audience listens to presentations? Of course they do. And you might have noticed something else about that list: all of the elements are negative.

So if audience members expect to be bored and carry all those negative expectations into your presentation, imagine their delight in the first seconds as you demonstrate by a strong opening that you will not be a typical, bland presenter. Your opening immediately carries you above expectations and thrills just about everyone.

3. A strong opening helps you overcome presentation anxiety.

Remember those awful few minutes just before you began your presentation? You know, when the audience was making its most critical value judgment of you? Great presenters don't have to deal with that. They have one job in the minutes before and during their introduction:

they mentally keep going
over the words to their memorized openings.

Great presenters know an elementary fact about how people think: you can only think of one thing at one time. In fact, if you're able to think of two things at the same time, you'll probably find large chapters in psychology textbooks devoted to you.

So while inexperienced presenters sit there quakin' and shakin' thinking, "Boy do I hate presentations! I just know I'll make a terrible ass of myself up there!" good presenters are going over their memorized openings and how they'll deliver them. They don't occupy their minds with negative thoughts because they can only think of one thing at a time and they're thinking about their openings.

Whom do you think has a better start?

What do you think about complete memorization?

Everyone has a horror story of watching some poor mope blank out during a speech and never saying another word until he's seated. I'm asked all the time how often

I've seen it. The answer is never. I'm sure it happens but I can honestly say I've never seen anyone stop dead, not utter another sound, and have to be helped from the stage with fixed, unseeing eyes.

Now, in truth, I must say, I've seen just about every other way one can stop a presentation dead. I've seen people faint, I've seen them burst into uncontrollable giggles and unstoppable crying jags, and, in all seriousness, I've seen a person literally have a heart attack upon being introduced. I've seen a fist fight between a presenter and someone who kept asking him rude questions and I've actually seen someone knock over a lectern and a microphone at the very same time (tee miny martoonies.) But in all the years I've watched speeches, I've never seen anyone stop dead and not be able to go on because he couldn't think of one more word to say. I hope I never do.

I bring up all of this (just in passing) to warn you against the dangers of memorization. There are only two elements in your presentation I would ever suggest you memorize: your opening and your closing. Neither should be more than 90-seconds long. That's it.

Because memorization works so well here (for many different reasons such as "opening minute anxiety"), inexperienced presenters think it will work well through their entire presentation. They're wrong (again, for many different reasons). When you memorize and deliver ideas, different thought processes and skills are involved than when you present ideas in the manner discussed in this book. And if the memorized train slips off the track, strange presenter reactions take place, a number of which I've cited above.

What do you think of jokes as strong openings?

If a joke is funny enough, clean enough, and relevant enough to tell an audience, chances are they've heard it. And if it's not any of these, chances are they don't want to hear it.

I make a clear distinction between jokes and humor. Humor classically and naturally rises from the situation or occasion. Jokes, on the other hand, are picked up somewhere else and pounded to fit the circumstance. Humor is great for presentations - if you do it well. If you are humorous, you know it by now and probably have for years. If you have any real doubts (beyond noble modesty) about your ability to recognize and deliver humor, you probably don't have enough to risk in front of an audience.

Sorry. I don't mean to sound harsh here but there's really nothing worse in presentations than very unfunny people trying to sound funny. The few laughs they receive are often more at their attempts at humor than the humor itself. To be a great presenter, you must turn up the volume on the strong, positive traits you have, not just what you think audiences want to hear. Besides, great presenters are not often measured by humor, they're measured in the communication traits that more commonly influence people: sincerity, passion, clarity, logic, openness, directness, and many others.

No jokes. No greetings.
What can I use for strong openings?

1. A dramatic statement.

The "in the time it took me to rise from that seat..." piece used by the research director is a great example of a dramatic statement opening. Dramatic statements must be forceful, clear, original, and hit the audience right in the intellectual guts. But be careful. They must not be threatening or belligerent.

"One person out of every four in this room will be the victim of a violent crime sometime in his or her lifetime," is an excellent dramatic statement opening.

"You or someone in your family will be a victim of a violent crime sometime in your lifetime," is not. The difference is truth and taste. The second statement may or may not be true. Of course the first statement may or may not be true also but audiences will grant that bit of "artistic license" so you can dramatically make your point. When it comes to threatening an audience member or, worse, an audience member's family, however, not only will you not be granted that license, you'll have become a most unpleasant person in the audience's eyes. This is certainly a difficult perspective from which to express your views regardless of how honorable they are.

2. A Rhetorical Question.

A rhetorical question does not require an answer because the answer is so obvious. It's asked for effect rather than for information or participation. Sometimes the presenter can give the answer himself to build a rapport with his audience. Here's an example,

"We all want a safe workplace for our people, don't we? Of course, we do!"

In this situation, the presenter is actually speaking for the audience. Of course he had better make sure what he says is what they really want to say. It's obvious in the example he has not overstepped his bounds; after all, what audience member would advocate an unsafe workplace?

In the opening above, an experienced presenter would "get 'em noddin'." This means he would speak for them and, literally, nod his head up and down to signify "yes." In most circumstances, a large number of audience members will nod their heads in agreement. Although they may be threatened by agreeing with the speaker verbally, often they feel they can support the point of view by a non-verbal gesture.

In this same vein, some professional speakers (none that

I know, of course) take the "get 'em noddin'" technique one step further. They know they can always "get a yes from the back row." This means that if they want some quick audience affirmation on a point, they can always pose a question, look above the heads of audience members, and to no one in particular, say something like "hasn't this happened to you sometime?"

They then look to the back row at a nonexistent audience member (who miraculously seems to be agreeing), and start nodding their own heads in reaffirmation of the "ghost" audience member's experience.

Of course the real audience members assume the presenter is getting agreement from someone back there and aren't about to take the trouble to turn around in their seats and check to see from whom.

Is this technique dishonest or immoral? Of course not. Look, we're not selling napalm here, I'm merely telling you some techniques some presenters use to establish a rapport with audiences. If the presenter "got agreement" on some particularly outlandish or weird point from an audience member, you can bet others would turn in their seats to see who the dolt in the back row was.

3. A Real Question.

"How many people here have thought about joining a union?"

Real questions are real risky in the hands of inexperienced presenters who like the technique but don't quite have the skill or experience to pull it off smoothly. There are two things you should know right away about using real questions as openings in your presentations.

The first is that if the question flops, that is, if you get a different response or no response from the audience, you look like an ass right away. That's a tough way to begin your presentation.

The second thing you should know is that in the beginning of your presentation, audiences are reluctant to commit to anything. I'm quite sure if you walked in front of an audience and began, "O.K. how many of you would like to live and see tomorrow?" less than half of the audience would raise their hands. It's not that they don't want to live, it's that they don't want to play - at least not yet.

Experienced presenters take advantage of the audience's natural reluctance to commit in the opening by reversing the question into a negative. The question then becomes, "Is there anyone here who would not like to live and see tomorrow?" Of course, most audience members aren't going to raise their hands in any case and it would take a real blockhead to raise his hand in answer to that particular question.

Unless you consider yourself an experienced presenter, know your audience and their anticipated reactions thoroughly, and feel like living on the wild side, I would forgo real questions as openers - they're just too risky in that first minute.

What's the best way to have
audience members raise their hands?

Even though "real question" openings aren't the best places to get audience members to raise their hands, there are parts in many presentations when this exercise is desirable. A question and answer period immediately comes to mind.

In any case, it's a good idea for you to make this request without sounding like an elementary school teacher. "If you want to ask a question, would you please raise your hand?" is a little clunky for any audience member over seven.

The best solution is elegantly simple and the groundwork has already been done for you. When it's time for audience participation, good presenters pose the question with one of their hands up - you don't have to mention the physical prerequisite at all. Here's the alternative to the example above: you say, "Any Questions?" with one of your hands raised. Audience members will get the idea.

4. A Personal Experience.

Even though the older, Texas gentleman was the head of a large trust foundation, when he stood before our small group, he looked sheepish. His assignment was to tell the audience why he was taking my seminar on effective presentations.

"When I wa-wa-was in the third grade," he slowly drawled, "I had to-to give a little ta-talk in front of the class. My teacher, Ma-ma-Mr. uh-Smith, was trying to teach me not to uh-stutter. He had a little sa-sa-squirt gun and uh-every time I uh-stuttered, he squirted me. Sa-some of the kids laughed and I ga-got pretty uh-wet but it didn't help."

My mouth was literally open with horror. I looked around the room at the seminar participants and their reactions were very much the same. If someone had yelled, "Let's tar and feather the bastard!" I'm sure we all would have fallen over each other barreling towards the door to find the long-dead Mr. Smith.

I love Texans! Nobody tells a personal experience opener better than my Texas friends. To me, Texans are like New York Italians with cowboy hats and boots. They're warm, and smart, and tough, and funny. Personally, I think Texas is still the biggest and best state in the union; any half-baked, "pretender to the Lone" is just dessert compared to the rich, grand dinner that's called Texas.

Audiences love personal experience openers. Perhaps it's because they're trying to establish a human rapport with the speaker or because they're so tired of trite, cliched beginnings, but in any case, a personal experience story is a sure winner as an opener if three standards are met: 1. it's relevant, 2. it's short, and 3. it doesn't make you the hero.

1. Relevancy is a very subjective area. What's relevant to some people often is not relevant to others. Because a personal experience is so, well, personal, there must be no question in your mind that every audience member immediately recognizes its relevance.

Relating a personal experience that misses its relevance target is worse than telling a "funny" story that isn't funny. If you miss with the funny story, you're just a typical, dull presenter; if you miss with the personal experience, you're a typical, dull presenter with an ego problem.

2. How quickly do you have to make your point? In about 90-seconds, just like any other opening. Remember, you're going to memorize it and deliver it in a memorable way. Don't start rambling about "the good old days," or spice your story with moralizing ("seems people cared more about each other back then") - you don't have the time and no one cares anyway. Just quickly make the point and please . . . .

3. Don't be a hero. If you rush into a burning building to save an old lady, you're a hero. If I tell someone you rushed into a burning building to save an old lady, you're a hero. If you tell someone you rushed into a burning building to save an old lady, you're an obnoxious braggart.

Personal experience openings should be relevant stories about how you felt or what you observed; things to which the audience can relate with empathy. They would love, for a few moments, to see the world from your eyes. But the situation dramatically changes when you make yourself the hero. Then they may rightfully question the integrity of the story, your taste in telling it, and why they have to listen to you "go on" about your greatness.

If the three guidelines of personal experience openers are met, they rank among the most powerful beginnings of great presentations.

5.   A "Slice-of-life."

A "slice of life" opening is a true story that does not star you. They're almost always popular with audiences. They have to meet the first two criteria of personal experience openers (1. relevancy and 2. under 90-seconds) but do not have to concern themselves with the ego/hero issue.

One of the best "slice-of-life" openers I heard kicked off a presentation about cutting through the bureaucracy of a large midwestern manufacturing firm.

It seems that the security department demanded chains be put on a certain set of exit doors because tools and goods were "walking" out of the plant. The local fire department understood the problem but understandably wouldn't consider allowing the doors to be chained without a very specific plan of exactly what would happen in case of fire.

A committee was formed and meetings went on forever about how many keys would have to be distributed and to whom and shouldn't everyone have a key and wouldn't that defeat the whole purpose and why not an expensive alarm system and new locks ad nauseum. As usual, the committee was going where most committees go: nowhere. Until one day when the problem was solved - neatly, cheaply, and anonymously.

When the workers arrived at the plant that day, resting on the chains was a large, gleaming bolt-cutter and a sign crudely painted in big, red letters. The sign said, "In case of fire, cut chains and open door."

You can see why audiences love slice-of-life stories. They're real, they're fast, and they make the point in a memorable way. When thinking of an opening, one of the first recesses in my mind I would check is the one that stores slices-of-life.

6. A Prop.

There's only one proper prop - the one that makes so much sense to use that no one can accuse you of indulging in "gimmickry." And when you use this rare find, you must use it correctly.

I've seen presenters do all sorts of things with props - most of which did not help their cause. I've seen them use props as pointers, as tools, as paperweights, even as back scratchers. New presenters drop props, leave them out far too long as tempting visual distractions, and sometimes have audience members pass them around. Sometimes the poor props don't make it back to the presenter in the same condition in which they left. Sometimes they don't make it back at all.

Years ago, I watched a narcotics enforcement presentation to young high school students. The officer sent around a prop that consisted of a cardboard display of all sorts of pills and other illegal "high-on-life" alternatives. As expected, he got about half of them back. Grinning like a smile button, he announced he had done that on purpose to show how stupid drug users are: all the samples were fake.

None of the kids laughed. Probably they were wondering (as I was) what overworked drone had to glue new fake samples to the prop board after each of Officer Grin's demonstrations. In this case, the prop had taken over too much of the presentation and it certainly wasn't helping achieve the assumed objective.

There's only one effective way to use a prop: conceal it, smoothly display it and make your point, and then conceal it again. When you know this is the only effective way to use a prop, you quickly eliminate a whole list of potential contenders including army tanks and live animals.

The most effective use of a prop I ever saw was demonstrated by the president of a small computer company on the West Coast. He had hired me to help him with his speaking skills but wanted to try out an opening in the privacy of a small banquet room before addressing the entire company. When I saw the professionalism of his prop opening, I inquired about taking some lessons from him!

It seems his company had fallen on some rough financial times and was looking to a "breakthrough" semiconductor product to save it. The president was to introduce this new product at a full gala meeting. When the dramatic moment arrived, he walked to center stage with an obvious bulge in his pocket and faced the cheering throng.

"I have in my pocket," he loudly announced, "the only invention that can turn this company around!" As the crowd began to cheer, he pulled out a large calculator! There was a gasp from the audience as the cheering faded out.

"The fine invention I'll introduce in a few minutes will be our breakthrough product - but if our company does not start doing a better job of calculating our expenses against anticipated revenue - no new product can ever save us!" He then put the calculator back in his pocket and went on with the rest of his presentation. Now that's what I call one hell of an opening!

If your prop makes so much sense that no one can call it a gimmick and you can use it correctly, it can be very effective in a strong opening.

• One quick note. You may run into some people (as I do) who priggishly say that the correct term for "props" is "visual aids." You may run into some who say that the correct term for "podium" is "lectern." And you may run into those who say that the plural of "communication" is "communication," not "communications." Although they may be technically correct, as far as I'm concerned, you may run into these people as many times as you like - preferably with a large truck or the tank you couldn't use as a prop.

Now you have a good half dozen proven, strong opening ideas. Work with them and make them work for you.

If you go through this list and still begin your presentation with "good morning, ladies and gentlemen," I can assure you, it won't be.

What do you think of using quotes to open a presentation?

Blah. Overdone. You can do better. See page 170.

What about dictionary definitions?

Double blah. These aren't even interesting in the dictionary.

I just feel comfortable saying "good morning" to my audience. Can I just say that and then deliver a strong opening?

It seems you want to greet that audience in the worst way - and the worst way may well be in the opening of your presentation. Of course you feel comfortable saying "good morning" to your audience. Everyone does - they've been doing it that same way for years. My purpose, however, is not to make you feel totally comfortable. My purpose is to make you totally effective and I can't imagine what "good morning" can possibly add to your presentation. IF IT DOESN'T ADD, IT SUBTRACTS.

Summary

Your opening is one of the most important elements of your presentation. You can never be a great presenter without understanding and mastering strong openings. The strong opening has three major objectives:

1. It immediately involves your audience in your subject matter.

2. It immediately distinguishes you from dull, common presenters. And,
3. It helps you overcome presentation anxiety.

Your opening is one of the few elements for which I suggest word for word memorization.

Although there are others, I've discussed six strong openings:

1. Dramatic statements.
2. Rhetorical questions.
3. Real questions.
4. Personal experiences.
5. Slices-of-life, and
6. Props.

If you're really pressed for time, the "objective as opening" technique I describe in my formula is adequate but certainly not as powerful as the ideas listed above. It does, however, beat "good morning, ladies and gentleman," every single time.

STEP 7
CHOOSE YOUR CONCLUSION

Why do presenters thank audience members at the end of their presentations?

If your opening was your first chance to distinguish yourself from other presenters, the conclusion is your last. Today, the vast majority of speeches end with a mumbled 'thank you' as relieved presenters sigh, gather their wrinkled papers and flopping visual aids, and shuffle back to their seats like they've just completed the most ordinary task in a most extraordinary way. In fact, they have accomplished neither.

Why do presenters thank audience members at the end of their presentations?

Some think I'm rude for even asking the question. "What do you mean, 'why do I thank my audience?' We've always done it that way. It's only polite."

Anyone who knows me knows I'll take a back seat to no one when it comes to manners in presentations. I'm happiest when presenters and audience members are behaving as civilized human beings in spirited discourse on the intellectual merits and rational stature of sound propositions. I just get snarly when presenters act like dimwits. And they act like dimwits when they parrot trite, mindless phrases which are neither appropriate for the occasion nor demonstrate the least amount of creative ingenuity.

Why do presenters thank audience members at the end of their presentations?

Usually presenters are thankful at the end of presentations - they're thankful they don't have to go through their self-imposed presentation agony any longer. But most tell me that's not the reason they thank audiences. They thank audiences for their time and attention.

Please think about that for a moment.

You should know that a presentation is a basic economic transaction between two parties: you as a presenter and your audience. Each of you hopes to get something of benefit from this exchange. Audience members aren't doing you a favor by listening to you - they hope to receive something of value from the experience.

You are not sacrificing time and effort out of the goodness of your heart, either. You're hoping to exchange these commodities to achieve an objective for your own benefit. Of course a good economic transaction must be a fair exchange; both parties should feel they benefit from the encounter.

This may seem to you like intellectual nitpicking but it's really not. If you think audiences are doing you a favor by listening to your presentation and you must thank them for it, you probably don't feel you have information, ideas or expertise of sufficient value to exchange. Now if you truly don't, you should thank audiences for giving up precious time to listen to your worthless babble - but if you do have a deserving presentation to deliver, they will be happy to listen.

If you get into the mind set that your audience members are doing you a favor by listening to your ideas, it will color your entire presentation. I've seen it on countless occasions: presenters, in a desperate attempt to please audience members, put themselves into all sorts of ingratiating positions reducing the inherent value of their ideas and themselves. They'll do anything to please audience members and virtually nothing to achieve their presentation objective - the only valid reason for speaking in the first place.

How do you know if you've been a gushing, boot-licking audience pleaser?

Here are a few quick signs:
  • you profusely thank everyone for giving you the wonderful opportunity to present that day.

- you tell them what a tremendous, nay, magnificent honor it is for little old you to present before such an esteemed, distinguished, highly regarded, much-lauded, blah-blah-blah group.
- you tell them you'll do the best you can to live up to their presentation expectations.
- you ask them if the visual aids / sound system / room temperature / lighting / etc. is all right.
- you apologize for: your lack of preparation / your visual aids / the cold you have that day / the dull information you must go over / the fact that you're taking up some of their oxygen.
- you thank them warmly and often at the end of your talk for having the benevolence to take some time out of their busy, important days to listen to your drivel.
- you offer to wash their cars on your days off and mow their lawns on holidays.

Do I exaggerate? Of course - to make a point. Yet I have heard every one of those points expressed - except the last (yet) by panicking presenters slavishly trying to please audience members. It's not a pretty sound.

How do audience's react? Predictably. They run all over the presenter. They often don't listen. They interrupt. They ask rude questions. They leave early. And they often demonstrate their disrespect in countless less subtle ways like talking to each other across the room or walking between the presenter and his audience to get a cup of coffee during the presentation.

Why should audience members respect a wimp presenter? The presenter has not demonstrated authority. The presenter obviously isn't confident in the worthiness of his ideas or his ability to present them. The presenter has put himself in a subservient position; he's forgotten that 'people treat you as you expect to be treated.' If you act like Rodney Dangerfield, don't expect to be treated like Jason Robards!

(By the way, if either of these gentlemen ever read this book, I'll be very honored. Certainly Mr. Robards might be flattered and Rodney - my favorite comedian - might be offended. BUT WHAT DOES HE EXPECT? . . . . . . .See what I mean?)

I'm not advocating an arrogant, insensitive, power-crazed presentation style. Not only would it be counterproductive, I personally would not like to work in a business - nor live in a world - where presentations like that were the norm.

I would like to see a world where civilized individual human beings could stand up and not feel embarrassed or inferior when they present their thinking and ideas to other human beings. A place where a person's self worth is not determined by the acceptance or rejection of his ideas by others. A world where everyone felt she or he could always present the best of herself or himself to wise, caring audiences - and maybe the people who took the trouble to read this book could do it all just a little bit better.

Holy mackerel! I just wanted a better way to end my talk! Did you get caught in a '60's time warp or what?

Sorry. One of the few things in life about which I feel passionate is the disrespect some people show for other people. When this happens to one of my presenters, even if he has allowed it to occur, I have been known to go off a bit.

What about my conclusion?

Right. Since your conclusion is your last chance to make an impression on your audience, it too must be distinctively different in a professional way. There's one main objective for all conclusions: to leave one last, powerful impression of you on audience members. Although the 'restated objective' conclusion cited in my formula is adequate for many presentations (and definitely superior to 'thank you'), there are much better ones.

Such as?

Surprise. All of the examples I went over for strong openings are equally appropriate for strong conclusions. See how easy this is? The examples were:

1. dramatic statements, 2. rhetorical questions, 3. real questions, 4. personal experiences, 5. slices-of-life, and 6. props. All of the same criteria and suggestions for each of the examples still apply for conclusions.

If I use one of these for my opening, can I still use one from the same category for my conclusion?

Sure. Your can use the same categories for your opening and closing or you can choose different ones. Personally I would try different categories (perhaps a dramatic statement opening and a slice-of-life closing), unless I was going to deliver the famous 'Open and Close Match.'

What's the 'Open and Close Match'?

You've probably heard this many times in presentations. The presenter relates (or "matches") the conclusion to the opening. Remember our dramatic statement opening example - the research director and the $2000 spent and $500 wasted (page 87)? He used this for his conclusion:
"During the brief time I've spent delivering this presentation to you, our company spent another $40,000 on re-

search and development. Once again, we may assume that over 10,000 of those dollars were wasted. How much longer can this company afford losses of that magnitude?"

And then he sat down.

Can the 'Open and Close Match' be from two different categories of openings and closings?

Of course. In the example above, the opening was a dramatic statement but the closing actually had a dramatic statement coupled with a rhetorical question. An 'open and close match' couples ideas, not categories - and no opening or closing always fits neatly into just one category.

What was the best 'Open and Close Match' you ever saw?

The research director's match was a real audience stopper but the best by far was used by the competitor who beat me for the national intercollegiate championship in persuasive speaking in the early 1970's.

The gentleman showed up in a bright red suit, white shoes, a wild tie and he spoke about gay rights. I believe his opening was something like, "When I dress like this, people assume I'm gay and the way they treat me is shocking." He then went on to talk about stereotypes, our treatment of fellow human beings, and the fact, of course, that liberal college students and professors like us could never be guilty of that insensitivity. His closing punched us right where it hurt.

"Many of you think you could not be guilty of the stereotyping and insensitivity of which I've spoken today. But I'd like to ask you two simple questions. First, as I stood here before you, how many times did you ask yourself, 'Is he gay?' And second, 'What does it matter to you?'"

Boooom! I felt like one of Mike Tyson's first opponents. Forevermore, I would be known as a distant 'Number Two.'

Was he gay?

What did it matter? He was a world class speaker that just beat the hell out of me; anything beyond that was his business, not mine.

Are closings as important as openings?

No. Openings are more important because of the audience's first impressions and the opening's ability to help reduce presentation anxiety. However, no great presenter ever misses an opportunity to distinguish himself from other presenters in a professional way. Strong closings present just such an opportunity.

Are there any closings that would be inappropriate as openings?

Well, certainly any one that begins, "Now that you've heard my presentation . . ." - that would confuse audience members. However, there are three closings that just seem to work better at the end of presentations.

I call the first, put yourself in the audiences' seat. As an example, let's say you've just finished a persuasive presentation to a potential new client who's auditioning advertising agencies to replace the one he now has. You might say,

"Well Jim, that just about concludes the formal presentation we've prepared for you. I know you have some hard decisions to make in the next few days. You're probably going to go back to your office right after this, sit back, and think about what you saw and what you felt during these talks.

If you do that and feel that we're the agency for you, just reach over, pick up the phone, and call us. We'll be waiting for your call and we'll be over within the hour to give you the type of service you deserve."

Why is this an effective conclusion?

Empathy; you're expressing concern for the audience member. You're not just presenting points you need to express - you're putting yourself in his position and trying to understand what he needs to do.

What are the other two conclusions?

"One more thing" and "ask for the order." Let's use our last example again.

One more thing.

"Jim, those are the three reasons you should choose Hutchicam Agency: 1. Creativity, 2. Cost, and 3. Consumer orientation. Now I know you've seen a lot of agencies this week and they're all probably starting to blur on you. Everyone probably has been telling you pretty much the same thing. Everyone is creative. Everyone is cost effective. And everyone has experience with consumer accounts."

"When you review Hutchicam's work however, I'd like you to think about one more thing: on average, our clients have stayed with us seven or eight years longer than clients have stayed with the other agencies you've seen. And there's only one reason that's so: we treat 'em right. We give 'em our best all the time. If you choose us, we'll do the same for you."

The one more thing conclusion should feature a brilliant piece of new information that goes beyond the solid case you made in the main presentation. The gem should be short, have some wallop, and be easy to remember.

The ask for the order conclusion is familiar to salespeople.

If done well, with the right circumstances, it can be a bold, confident end to a presentation. If it's forced (that is, if the audience member has no intention of signing that day or even if he did, he wouldn't sign with you or he fell asleep during your talk or left the room or got sick on your shoes) the presenter comes across like a twerp. Here's the example,

"Jim, those are the three reasons you should choose Hutchicam Agency: 1. Creativity, 2. Cost, and 3. Consumer orientation. We know we can do the job for you. When do we begin?" or "How soon can we get started?" or "Is there anything else you need to know before you hire us?"

One disadvantage of the ask for the order conclusion is that you have to 'read' your audience throughout your presentation and abandon the approach if the outcome doesn't look promising. Obviously, you must make this decision during the presentation (sometimes difficult with team presentations) and you must have a backup plan.

Do professional presenters have "canned" openings and closings or do they create new ones for each audience?

All of the above. Professional presenters usually have canned everything which they masterfully (one hopes) adapt to each audience. If we're good, the audience never sees the "seams" (the new elements and transitions "stitched" to the old).

One technique professional presenters exercise to great advantage, especially in openings and closings, is the pause.

Doesn't every presenter pause?

Not on purpose. Not for dramatic effect. Most new presenters horrifyingly experience pauses as one second from black out and two seconds to brain dead. They would never think to stop on purpose. That's why they often speak so quickly and stuff their pauses with "uhs," and "ya knows."

Great presenters know that effective pauses are one of strongest means they have to command and focus an audience's attention. When a presenter is first introduced, those first few seconds can be a little loose. Some people may still be talking or applauding the introduction. The person who introduced him may be making his way back to his seat (seemingly never in an unobtrusive manner). All sorts of things are usually going on.

As soon as he's in his speaking position, the experienced presenter will look the room over, smile at the audience, and then wait for a full count of two (one-thousand one, one-thousand two) before beginning. As strange as this may sound to you, those two seconds make a tremendous difference.

That pause can command an audience's attention. They expect immediate sound. When they don't hear it, their attention is primed. When the next sound they hear is the beginning of a strong opening presented by a compelling voice, the effect can be electrifying.

The two second pause is also used by great presenters in their closings. Inexperienced presenters sometimes deliver their closings (and their thank you's) as they hurry towards their seats. Whooosh - they're gone! They can't wait to get away. Experienced presenters slow down on their last few words, focus on their most important audience member (or someone who is in the middle of their audience) and, when they conclude, they "freeze" and hold for a count of two. The effect is dramatic.

I'll say it's dramatic! It sure wouldn't be appropriate for me.

Two things. First, when you isolate and put into words some rather subtle presentation devices (like this one) a lot gets lost in the translation. What starts as a sophisticated, natural-appearing technique that quickly and effectively glides by an audience in person seems to become a rather clunky, artificial stage trick best left to a select group of religious evangelists. In reality, this is not the case at all. I would guess you've seen appropriate dramatic pauses in virtually every one of the memorable presentations you've witnessed - you just weren't aware of the technique.

Second, how could you possibly know if this technique, or any other I've suggested in this book, is appropriate for you or not until you've thought about it with an open mind, rehearsed it thoroughly, and then tried it out a few times on live audiences to gauge its effects?

For having a closed mind on presentations, you are sentenced to read "Excuses" (page 175) and to close each of your next three presentations with "Thank you," even though you now know how trite and dull it makes you sound.

Summary

The purpose of a closing or conclusion is to leave one strong lasting impression of you on your audience members. Although not as important as openings, closings still provide excellent opportunities for great presenters to separate themselves from the large, dull "heard."

The six examples of openings are all appropriate for closings. In addition, there are a number of others you can choose. One is called the 'Open and Close Match' where you couple or 'match' ideas from your opening to your closing. The others comprise a small category of three ideas which are best suited to closings: 1. put yourself in the audience's seat, 2. one more thing, and 3. ask for the order.

Each of these choices has advantages and disadvantages determined by your specific presentation and objective.

For a closing, "real" presenters don't say thank you.

PREVIEW • GO THROUGH • REVIEW

Who first said, "tell 'em what you're gonna tell 'em - tell 'em - and then tell 'em what you told 'em"?

I have no idea.   I doubt if it was Demosthenes, the famous Greek orator.   Best known for stuffing pebbles into his mouth to stop his stammer, Demosthenes attributed his presentation greatness to extensive, arduous rehearsal. So he would not be tempted to cut into his precious rehearsal time, he would often shave one half of his head appearing too ridiculous to consider leaving home.

Demosthenes doesn't strike me as a "tell 'em what you're gonna tell 'em" kind of guy.

Actually, aside from its dubious grammar, use of slang, and silly sing-song cadence, "tell 'em, etc." is very good presentation advice. It underscores the strong structure and repetition about which I am so adamant. It also leads to a smooth approach for transitions which can be valuable for presenters. More on that in a moment.

My seminars and lectures are far too expensive for me to simply reheat old chestnuts like "tell 'em, etc." So I call the technique, preview • go through • review. See the expensive difference? (I love the story about Albert Einstein and the reporter who asked him if he carried around a notebook to jot down all his new ideas. "Actually," replied Einstein, "I don't get too many new ideas.")

Much of my simple presentation formula is actually a modification of this old idea. In the formula, a few given words plus the preview step form the opening. After adding the objective, the go-through step becomes the body of the talk. Finally, a few pat words plus the review step and the objective make up the closing.

Since you've come this far in the book, I'll assume you'd like to go beyond the basic formula for a great presentation. Preview • Go through • Review is a good place to begin. Some simple explanation is in order first.

Preview and review for our purpose, are exactly the same things: a very limited number of simple, numbered points which answer your objective. Their only difference is when they occur in your presentation. The preview step is delivered before the main body and the review step follows it.

The go-through step, not surprisingly, is where you go through the explanation of your numbered points. It is the main body of your presentation. Here's how the complete presentation looks in outline form:

A. Opening
B. Objective
C. PREVIEW
D. GO-THROUGH
E. REVIEW
F. Closing

Let's use an example. We start with the objective - always. (Remember? Simple, clear, one sentence long.) My objective is "to explain my job to my audience." Since I have a limited amount of time, I will focus only on the two main elements of my job and limit each of those to two words. When I've completed this short task, the preview and review are done.

My next step is to expand upon those points (with as little detail as I need) to complete my go-through step. Here's our outline again, now using the example:

A. Opening   (To be decided.)
B. Objective: "To explain my job to my audience."
C. Preview: 1. Delivering seminars.
   2. Delivering presentations.
D. Go-through: 1. Delivering seminars.
   (Here I start filling in a limited number of details to explain this point.)

                 2. Delivering presentations. (Same as above.)

E. Review: 1. Delivering seminars.
                         2. Delivering presentations.

F. Closing   (To be decided.)

Out loud, after my strong opening, it will sound something like this:

"My objective today is to explain my job to you. My job has two major components. Number one, delivering seminars and number two, delivering presentations. (Pause for one second.) Number one, delivering seminars. My seminars have taken me blah, blah." (Here's where I fill in the necessary details to make those points and fit within my allotted time. When finished explaining point two, I pause for one second and then launch into the Review step.)

"So those are the two elements of my job: number one, delivering seminars and number two, delivering presentations." (I would pause for a second and then deliver my boffo closing.)

Compare this structure, simplicity, and repetition with the last few hundred presentations you've heard. As an audience member, which would you be more likely to listen to and remember?

Won't audience members become insulted or bored when you make things that simple and repeat them so often?

Absolutely not! When you repeat something three times to most audience members, they're usually just on the threshold of understanding. Remember, they're not reading for information, they're listening for information and they need it this simple and repeated often

Also, once again, remember that isolating these techniques and putting them into written words makes them appear much more prominent than they do when heard by audience members. What may read like laborious repetition to you, speeds by within seconds during an actual presentation.

How can "preview, • etc." help with transitions?

New presenters often have tough times with transitions. They just don't know what to say when they shift to different sections of their presentation. It often comes out like, "Now I'm going to talk about . . ." or "Switching gears for a minute . . ."

When they follow the simple format I've suggested here, the problem is eliminated. The structure is so refined, the presenter merely has to pause rather than speak to go on to the next section. When the audience hears that "number one" again, after a pause, they know where they are in the talk. In affect, the presenter is "speaking an outline" which is very easy for audiences to follow.

When do I create the opening and closing?

When everything else is in place. You must always create presentations in a different order than you deliver them (assuming you're going to speak in an accepted, logical manner). The objective must always be written first. Next, create the points that answer the "why" or the "what" of the objective. Finally, compose the opening and closing. I suggest the opening should be created first because you may be able to "match" a strong closing to it.

Can this format help me
create my opening?

Absolutely.   Once your structure is firmly in place, mentally "step back" from it and try to "see it" for the first time, perhaps as a child. What jumps out from your presentation? What's the most important thing about it? Try to quickly form one, clear idea or impression that answers these questions.

When you've formed one, refer back to the half-dozen strong openings on page 91. Which one could best establish this one idea quickly and powerfully in your audience's mind? Keep working with the list. Try out different ideas.

Let's use as an example the outline that "explains my job." One thing that quickly emerges from "1. delivering seminars, and 2. delivering presentations," is that I talk a lot (some say I talk too much). How can I creatively and powerfully thump my audience with this fact in less than 90-seconds? What about a dramatic statement? How about this for an opening:

"You and I have many things in common. One of those is that we all like to talk. But in this sense, I'm very fortunate. You see when I talk . . . I get paid for it."

Stop snickering! I know that's no barn burner but I'm just trying to demonstrate a method that might help you get from your Preview • Go Through • Review structure to that format plus your opening and closing. Give me a break!

STEP 8
STOP WORRYING.

This step, perhaps more than any other, shows the clear distinction between making one great presentation and becoming a great presenter. It's represented by the significant difference between "acting unafraid" and "being unafraid" and the costs involved in both.

There will be many presentation purists who'll say the formula I've given you to make one, great presentation is superficial, may suppress your creativity, and robs you of the privilege of being forced to learn the history, art, and science of oratory - one of the most noble endeavors of civilized man.

They'll probably call my formula things like "McSpeech" and lament that the people who do deliver great presentations using my technique, will merely be actors with scripts who probably haven't learned much about the basic fundamentals of communication.

They're right, of course.

The purists and I disagree most critically in only one regard: they demand you become a great presenter first (with all the knowledge and skill that involves) before you deliver a great presentation. I've approached the situation from the opposite direction. I feel many of you will aspire to be great presenters (again, with all the knowledge and skill that involves) only after you experience the joy of making a great presentation.

As I've said, there are over 300 publications on public speaking in print today. They range from the driest post graduate communication theories to the glitziest "celebrity-written" bromides published by major publishing conglomerates. I've read many of them. Besides lacking a clear, simple formula for making one great presentation, many lack something else perhaps even more important:

> the joy and excitement one experiences
> from delivering a great presentation!

In an increasingly depersonalized world, presentations are one of the last arenas where your fellow human beings become quiet for a moment, briefly suspend their attention to most other things, and focus on the person and ideas that are uniquely you. If you're like most people, you've probably never experienced the joy of presentations. You've probably never relaxed enough to calmly look around the room and savor the reactions of your audience members as they discover new ideas and new ways to look at the world from your perspective.

You've probably never had the pleasure of making an audience laugh or helping them see themselves in a different way. You've probably never been delighted by their smiles and applause or encouraged by their their thumbs-up signs. Of course, you've probably never had to continue when an audience member throws a different finger far into the air either - but that's exciting too! (This single digit gesture seems to bring out a hidden human streak in some otherwise dull, gray presenters. When it happens to George Bush, he reportedly quips, "Ah, another supporter who thinks I'm number one!" Once, during one of his presentations, Nelson Rockefeller received the same tribute and was so moved - he returned the gesture!)

In your presentations you've probably experienced excitement as anxiety, challenge as adversity, and opportunity as a thankless grind. As a tribute to presentations, how many antacids have you crunched? How many drinks have you slugged or nights have you lain awake dreading the dawn? How many shirts have you sweated through or nails have you bitten?

It's all such a terrific waste of what could be an exciting part of your life. You can become a great presenter, you know. You can't do it by delivering one great presentation but you can do it. Take a look around. Who's your competition? Do they present with imagination, power, and inspiration? Do they have any fun in their talks? Or do they look and sound pretty much like you?

I want you to succeed! I want you to be a great presenter! I want you to have fun, deliver your ideas with clarity, authority, and excitement, and I want you to move people - not information. I want all of these things for you . . . .and I don't even know you! But before you start achieving these things, you've got to stop being afraid of presentations.

If you've delivered a presentation and are still alive to read this book, you know presentations are not always fatal. If you've seen lots of presentations in your lifetime, you know that they're "almost never" fatal (I was taught never to say never). Your chances of getting struck by lightning are better than having anything horrendous happen to you in a presentation! Your chances of picking up Madonna hitchhiking are better! Your chances of being waited on by Mel Gibson in a convenience store are better!

I've had enough experience in presentations to know that's all true. I've also had enough experience to know that knowledge won't help you feel one little bit better.

The cost of presentation anxiety is high. You pay for it with stomach acid, sleepless nights, and dread. Worse, you pay for it by not attempting the strong presentation skills you've learned to make you "distinctively different in a professional way."

If you're in a meeting and five people stand up to deliver their presentations before you and each of them begins their talk with, "Good morning, ladies and gentlemen. My name is," - what are you going to do? What are you going to do even if you have a super opening that will kick off a great presentation?

If the acid is pumping into your stomach, and the "might-make-an-ass-of-myself" sentences are bouncing around your brain like hard hit ping pong balls, and every eye in the place is on you - you KNOW what you'll do - you dog, you - you KNOW what you'll do!

You'll spinelessly mope up to that lectern, white-knuckle it, and in a tight, tinny voice croak, "Good morning, ladies and gentlemen . . . . ."

Ohhhhhhhhhhhhhhhhhh.

You could have been somebody. You could have been a contender! But your presentation anxiety bought you a one way ticket to palookaville! When you sheepishly gaze around the auditorium from your podium hiding place, you see the dulled, glazed looks of those few audience members still awake - and you feel like pond scum.

Holy mackerel! What's the matter with you? I came to this section to learn how not to be afraid — not to hear you flake out!

Sorry. My apologies. To make up for that last little burst of craziness, I'll work extra hard to give you an antidote for presentation anxiety that will be worth many times the cost of this book. The homework will be simple, the technique easy to learn, and since I've taught this same basic lesson to over 3000 of my students with excellent results, I can guarantee it will work for you - if you use it.

It sounds hard already. Can't I just pinch my fingers together or take a pill?

I wish it was that easy but it's not (see Dumb Presentation Advice, page 162). What I'm going to teach you now is based on *A New Guide to Rational Living*, (Ellis and Harper, 1975) coauthored by the noted psychologist, Dr. Albert Ellis. The book does not deal specifically with presentation anxiety but I've used it to form a strategy of relief for my presenters who suffer from the hindrance (which includes just about all of them).

Very simply, Ellis's theory states, how you feel about certain events is largely determined by how you think about them, either consciously or subconsciously.

[If you are not the least bit interested in the background on why this method works so well with presentation anxiety, you may immediately turn to page 139 to begin thinking about your anxiety strategy before your next presentation.

The analogy here is that of the difference between using a simple formula to make a great presentation or learning how to become a great presenter. The anxiety "formula" will work quite well on its own - but you won't understand why - and everyone who does will laugh at you.]

When Ellis's idea is explained further, (although I'm hardly doing justice to his brilliance with this brief account) the process looks like this:

1. There's an activating event   (in our case, your presentation),
2. Which is influenced by your thought process and self-talk; here called your belief system. Which determines your:
3. emotional consequence (in our case, your presentation anxiety).

Why is this significant?

Because you've probably thought your whole life that activating events themselves determine emotional consequences and there's little you can do about that situation. You feel the way you do and that's that. When you understand that it's your belief system that's responsible for your emotional consequence, not the event itself, you realize you can do something about that.

Is it easy to change my belief system?

It's a lot easier than changing the events. In our case, it's a whole lot easier to change the way you think about presentations and how you talk to yourself about them rather than try to fix it so you'll never have to give another one.

I still question if activating events themselves don't have more to do with the emotional consequence than you're letting on.

Let's take an example. Say your dog Spot dies and you feel terrible. What's really causing your sadness is how you think and talk to yourself about Spot's death. It would probably go something like this:

1. Activating event: Spot's death.
2. Your belief system or self talk about the death:
     "I'll miss Spot."
     "Spot was the best dog I ever had."
     "Spot's death reminds me that some day I'll die."
3. Emotional consequence: sadness.

Doesn't everyone feel the same way?

Of course not. Even you wouldn't feel the same way if you had a different belief system about Spot. Let's say Spot wasn't your dog but your wife's dog and you always disliked the mutt anyway. Now let's look at our example:

1. Activating event: (the same) Spot's death.
2. Your belief system or self talk about the death:
    "No more Spot flops on the lawn."
    "No more Spot hairs on the furniture."
    "Maybe my mate will now give me some
    of the attention she used to give Spot."
3. Emotional consequence: happiness; contentment.

So you can see activating events themselves cannot cause emotional consequences. It's only how you think and talk to yourself about them.

What does this have to do with my presentation anxiety?

Everything. Now you can never say, "presentations make me afraid." You can only say, "I make myself afraid about presentations."

How do I do that?

By saying dumb things to yourself about your presentation, its importance, and the horrible things that will happen if you don't live up to your own (probably) unrealistic expectations about your performance. Even if you're saying these things to yourself at a subconscious level, the effect is still significant.

When we get to this point in my seminars, I ask my participants to repeat or paraphrase the sentences or thoughts that made them so afraid of that morning's relatively nonthreatening presentation. Wherever I go, I'm rarely surprised by the sentences; the words are remarkably similar,

"I hate presentations."
"I've never done well in presentations."
"What if I screw up bad?"

"What if I screw up in front of my peers? my boss? my
   employees?"
"I hate presentations."
"I always feel nervous in front of people."
"What if I faint?" (Have you ever fainted in a presenta-
   tion?) "No but there's always a first time!"
"I don't think I do it right."
"I don't think I do it well."
"Somebody told me I sound like a bird." (Sing like a
   bird?) "No.
 Sound like a bird." (Who told you that?) "I forgot -
   that was 30 years ago."
"Here goes nothing."
"Can I speak from my seat?"
"Would you turn around? Could everyone just turn
   around?"
"I hate presentations."
"I always feel like a fool."
"I always feel like my fly's undone."
"Everyone's watching me."   And, my all time favorite,
"Did you ever have to coach anyone as bad as me?"

The sentences aren't really funny to me anymore. I see
   the fear in my presenters' eyes. They've beaten themselves senseless with this nonsense and yet they know
   "intellectually" there's nothing to fear - they're just
   confused about why they're scared to death.
Two things on which I know every group will be "experts" are the above sentences and the physical symptoms of presentation fear:

"My mouth gets dry. Is that normal?"
"I have too much saliva - I think I'm spitting on the
   audience."
"I crash into things."
"My eyes twitch. Is that normal?"

"I get rashes... get flushes.....get hives."

"I turn red."

"My fingers shake."

"Did you ever coach anyone who's (fingers) (arms) (stomach) shakes?"

"Do a lot of people feel funny in their stomach when they speak?

(Butterflies?) "No, nausea."

"When your facial muscles tighten, don't your lips pull harder against your teeth?"

It's all so unnecessary. But instead of getting to the cause of their anxiety (their own belief systems about presentations) and curing it, my presenters come up with the some of the strangest temporary band-aids ever devised. These are my two favorites:

"If I talk softer, people won't hear my accent." and, "I guess I think if I stoop, people won't see me shake as much. Well, you're laughing but you noticed my stoop, not my shaking, right?"

How do you "cure" these problems?

These aren't problems; they're symptoms of the problem and the problem is an irrational fear of presentations. Once you "cure" that, you'd be amazed at how many symptoms disappear.

How do you "cure" my irrational fear of presentations?

Hey, I'm not going to cure your fear - I've got my own problems. You're going to cure it with some knowledge, a few simple exercises, and a consistent, systematic approach based on Ellis's principles. Here goes:

For our purposes, let's assume you have an important

presentation coming up next week. It's usually important to have a motivater like that. Now take out a calender and mark off five days before your presentation. You're going to do a simple "thinking" exercise for five minutes in the morning and five minutes at night for each of the five days preceding your talk.

What's the magic around the number five?

There's no magic. Any systematic approach would work but this combination seems to work better for most people when they exercise with their reality sentences.

What are reality sentences?

Reality sentences are statements we know to be true; not what we hope will be true or fear will be true; what we know to be true. Reality sentences are the most important part of my anxiety-reducing exercises. Although not directly from Ellis's R.E.T. work, his ideas formed the inspiration and basis for their creation. These sentences must make logical sense to you and you must believe in their "reality" as strongly as you believe that you've been breathing for the last few minutes.

Here's the first example of a presentation reality sentence:

• Generally, the audience wants me to do O.K.

Absolutely true? Of course it is. Now they may not buy what you wish to sell or accept each of your ideas but basically they want you to get through the presentation without undue stress or harm. At this point in my seminars, someone usually tries to shoot down the "reality" of the sentence by remembering some obscure incident that happened about a hundred years ago.

"Wait a minute," he'll blat, "I remember once in '65 when Harry Hoe glared at me throughout my talk because I walked out on his and he wanted me to fail."

The questioner forgot the modifier "generally." Even though he may remember a strange incident or two (and so can you), you must agree that most audiences most times want you to do O.K. - that's reality for most people.

Here's another presentation reality sentence:

• Basically, I know more about my subject matter than anyone in my audience.

I certainly hope this is true. If it's not, why are you presenting that day? Once again, the qualifier makes it virtual reality for most people all of the time.

Finally,

• Generally, I know about what I want to say and how I want to say it.

Once again, you may not know every single word you're going to say but generally you have a pretty good idea. After you've finished the rehearsal step in the next section, I guarantee this sentence will be true for you.

These sentences seem pretty boring.

Of course they're boring - they're just plain reality stripped of hopes and fears and fantasies. Reality is often boring - that's why they invented drugs and alcohol. But these dull sentences are exciting because they can lead you from the frightful fog of presentation anxiety.

Now what?

1. Copy the three reality sentences on a 3"x 5" or 4"x 6" card.

Here they are again:

· Generally, the audience wants me to do O.K.
· Basically, I know more about my subject than anyone in my audience.
· Generally, I know about what I want to say and how I want to say it.

2. Pick a place.
   Find a quiet place in your home and stand in a corner facing the walls for fewer distractions.

3. Fantasize the presentation environment.
   Imagine the room in which you'll speak five days from now. Make this fantasy as real as you can. Picture the audience, the chairs, and even what you'll wear that day. Imagine the notes in your   hand and the front of the room or lectern from which you'll speak. Even if you don't know all of these things, imagine them the best you can.

4. Feel the presentation anxiety.
   Now imagine it's just moments before you're to stand and speak. Feel your nervousness welling up inside. Welcome the unwelcome guest with all of his physical-symptom friends: the increased heartbeat, the sweaty palms, the tightened muscles. They're all here! The better you were able to recreate the presentation situation in your mind, the more Anxiety, Inc. will invade your body - and that's good. Now we'll start to deal with them in an impressive way without the distraction of presenting before a live audience.

5. Understand what's making you afraid.
   Why are you feeling anxious right now in your rec-

reated presentation situation? Think of it! There's nobody here - you're standing in a corner with your eyes closed surrounded only by your own strange thoughts and you feel afraid! The presentation's not making you afraid - there is no presentation! The audience is not making you afraid - there is no audience!

What's making you afraid? You're making yourself afraid with your own irrational sentences of which you may not even be aware. Sentences like, "I might make an ass of myself up here. I hate presentations! I'd feel like a horrible worm if I did lousy in this talk!" This is what's making you afraid, friend, and now we're going to do something about it.

How?

6. Read and reread the card of reality sentences.
   You thought your way into this mess, now think and talk your way out. You know what caused the fear but you don't know if your irrational sentences are true. You don't know if you're going to make an ass of yourself (whatever that means - after all, would you make an ass of yourself to every single audience member forever from this one speech?) but you do know:

   1. Generally, the audience wants me to do O.K.
   2. Basically, I know more about my subject than anyone in my audience.
   3. Generally, I know about what I want to say and how I want to say it.

   You know these things because they're true and you thought them through. The beauty of Ellis's principles is that human beings respond more powerfully to rationality than to irrationality. The sentences make sense to you and help push out the irrational fear.

Eventually, with the systematic approach I've described, your presentation reality sentences will replace your irrational ones at a subconscious level and your anxiety will be greatly reduced.

C'mon!

It's true. Aside from my individual coaching, the module in my seminars which has received the most amount of positive feedback over the years is this simple exercise for the reduction of presentation anxiety. The people who employ it are surprised when it works the first time but they keep at it and their presentations may actually become enjoyable. Sometimes the exercise works too well.

What do you mean?

It seems I'm always getting calls from people about the third or fourth day in their five day program and they usually sound something like this:

Caller: "Those sentences were good for about two or three days but now the exercise is becoming so boring, I'm having a hard time recreating my anxiety."
Me: "Why do you think you're having trouble recreating your anxiety?"
Caller: "Because I'm bored with the exercise."
Me: "Could there be another reason?"
Caller: "Like what?"
Me: "You figure it out. What caused your fear in the first place?"

Caller: "My irrational presentation sentences."
Me: "And if it's harder to recreate that fear now, what could be withering away like a plant without water?"
Caller: "My irrational presentation sentences? Wow! But what's doing that?"
Me: "I think it's either magic or the reality sentences."
Caller: (laughing) "Well I don't believe in magic."
Me: "Must be the sentences."
Caller: "Should I keep doing the sentences?"
Me: "Either that or start believing in magic."

A Quick Review

1. Copy your reality sentences on to a 3"x 5" card.
2. Pick a quiet place.
3. Fantasize the presentation environment.
4. Feel the presentation anxiety.
5. Understand what's making you afraid.
6. Think and talk yourself out of it by reading the sentences to yourself.

There's no particular way you're supposed to "feel" during this exercise, just do it five minutes twice a day for five days before your presentation. Make sure you don't stop on the third or fourth day when it gets harder to recreate your anxiety. That's an indication the technique is working.

What if presentations still make me scared?

Good presenters are never "scared" of presentations - they're excited about them. And of course presentations can't make you scared, remember? You do that to yourself.

It's important for you to stop reinforcing your fear by sentences like these. We've already seen how powerful sentences can be and how much they can affect your presentation anxiety. If you're serious about reducing your anxiety, you must start talking to yourself about it like a rational adult.

O.K. — what if the five day exercise didn't eliminate all of my presentation anxiety. What if I'm still too "excited"?

The exercise is not intended to eradicate your presentation anxiety completely. If it did that, I never would suggest it in the first place. A certain amount of controllable nervous energy is necessary for a great presentation. It's absolutely essential!

If you deliver your presentation like you're ordering a set of parts for your furnace, it's going to sound awfully dull. If you become so relaxed that there's no excitement in your voice, the talk will drag like a sack of potatoes.

Take that controlled amount of energy and rechannel it into some positive presentation techniques. We'll learn how to do that better in the next step on rehearsal. For now, don't think of it as a negative. Think of it as an essential ally.

In addition to the reality-sentences exercise, what else should I do about my presentation excitement?

Obviously, reality sentences have to be practiced long in advance of your presentation. There are two techniques I'll recommend that can be used just prior to or during your actual presentation.

During the presentation?

Sure. Any number of things happen to presenters during presentations which can trigger an attack of Anxiety, Inc. Rude questions, a waiter dropping a tray, the lights going out, a heckler, a fight breaking out, a projector bulb blows. When events like these explode, Anxiety, Inc. shoots into the fracas with adrenalin, a racing heart, and enough sweat and saliva to launch an armada. Reality sentences can not prepare you for an unexpected burst of unpleasantness.

What can I do?

First off, let's understand how a presentation surprise can trigger a physical but not necessarily a psychological reaction.

When a fear stimulus bursts into our consciousness, ("Frankly, those figures you just delivered are completely false and I can prove it. You're either a liar or a fool!") our bodies react in microseconds.

From ten million years of evolution to the famous "flight or fight" response, our bodies instantly react to danger in very physical ways: muscles tighten, adrenalin rushes into the system, breathing becomes rapid, *thought is suppressed,* and we instinctively react to the situation.

Thought is suppressed?

Of course. It has to be. Think of this: (not that this would ever happen to you but just pretend) say you're walking down a bad street at night, in a bad part of town, in a bad condition, and someone lurches out of the shadows at you. Do you react instinctively or do you go through the following thought process, "This surprise is probably dangerous but I know in this state I'm only allowed to use a reasonable amount of force to stem an attacker. I probably should look to see if he has a weapon . . . . or should I just run and try to get away?"

I'd react instinctively, obviously.

Of course you would! You'd be sidewalk meat before you got even halfway through your thought process. So in a fear stimulus reaction, your thought process is suppressed.

What does this have to
with presentations?

Too much. When your fight or flight response is triggered during a presentation ("Frankly, those figures . . . .") your ability to think of an appropriate response is severely hampered by the surge of physical defense symptoms rushing to your aid. What may have been life-saving on the sidewalk is now a burden as you face an audience.

Is there anything I can do?

Well of course there is - I wouldn't have brought it up if there wasn't! First, recognize that your body is doing what it's supposed to do - it's not working against you. Second, realize you're going to have to manually override your body's automatic physical response to begin thinking well again and meet the lout's challenge.

How can I do that?

Two quick ways. You must train yourself in these situations to immediately:

1. relax your shoulders, and
2. breathe deeply.

Relax my shoulders?

In a fear response, the muscles that get tightest fastest are the neck and shoulder muscles. Think of walking in a rainstorm with a group of people. When lightening flashes, people instinctively tighten their neck and shoulder muscles to protect their heads. Although that mini-inch duck is certainly an admirable endeavor when trying to save your life and continue the species, it undoubtedly has no effect if that bolt has your name on it.

In any case, relaxing your neck and shoulder muscles in a presentation gives you more control over the physical symptoms of fear triggered by an unpleasant surprise - as does deep breathing.

The breathing response to fear is short, quick breaths. This is great for karate yells at sidewalk assailants but doesn't translate well into presentation settings.

When do I use these techniques?

Anytime nervousness threatens your presentation. Some of my seminar participants have become very good at training themselves to respond to virtually every unusual presentation situation with these exercises - from questions to electronic crashes. Since they know they work, they also take comfort in the fact they can use them at will and aren't at the mercy of physical reactions.

Reality-sentence exercises before, the shoulder drop and deep breathing routine during, anything else?

We've already talked about our "first minute memorized opening" that gets my presenters off to a good start. In the next section I'll discuss rehearsal which is a key to not being overly "excited." Aside from this, I would recommend a healthy dose of common sense.

What do you mean?

I love it when I arrive at one of my seminars and the participants are speeding around feeding on each others' fear ("Boy, do I hate this!" "Me, too!" "I'm so nervous I might choke!" "You too? I'm so nervous, I might choke you!" "Feel my heart. Feel my heart!") Of course, all this inane chatter is sped along by the countless number of cups of coffee they've been drinking for hours. By the time they get in front of the class, their eyes look like unblinking, empty plates and they're machine gunning us at about 400 words per minute. I'm usually exhausted before they sit down!

You mean I shouldn't talk to my friends or drink coffee before a presentation?

I don't care what you do before your presentation - I don't even know you. But if you have a problem with presentation anxiety, it might be a good idea to cut back on your caffeine and not talk to your friends about nervousness. Anyway, besides you, whom do you think cares about your nervousness?   Your audience doesn't.

What!?

Sorry but we know that audience members are only initially sympathetic to nervous presenters. After that they become resentful because they certainly don't want to feel responsible for another person's pain - especially since they're not actively doing anything to cause that pain.

That thought makes me even more nervous!

Good. Now maybe you'll be even more motivated to eliminate irrational presentation fear and get on with the business of presenting yourself.

I don't want to see you afraid. I want to see you become a great presenter! And you can't do that until you start attacking your fear.

An anxiety-reducing strategy

There's a terrible cost to presentation anxiety. You've already bought the erroneous idea that "presentations make me afraid," - now you're going to have to pay for it. You can pay for it in ulcers, misery, and dull presentation techniques designed to relieve all pressure on you and render you instantly forgettable or you can use your intelligence and discipline to work with the following presentation anxiety-reducing strategy.

1. One week before your presentation:
   • outline your objective and main points (Steps 2 & 3 of formula) and create your Opening.
   • begin to memorize your Opening, word for word, out loud.

2. Five days before your presentation:
   • begin 5-minutes/twice per day Presentation Reality Sentences exercise.
   • continue exercise despite difficulty of recreating anxiety

3. The night before your presentation:
   • get a good night's sleep.
   • every time you have a moment of dread, immediately go over your Presentation Reality Sentences - every single time. You have control over your fear - use it! Fearing something that's not truly fearful becomes boring very quickly when you immediately and consistently answer the fear with rational thought. Do not wallow in your fear or think about things that *might possibly* happen - they won't!
   • fantasize about the positive highlights of your presentation: your strong opening, clear points, looks of respect on your audience member's faces when they

realize this is an outstanding presentation. Have confidence in your presentation!

4. The day of your presentation:
   • reduce or eliminate caffeine intake.
   • refuse to discuss with anyone (including family, friends, and strangers on the bus) any nervousness concerning your presentation. Remember the "I'm excited!" line and then smile.

5. Minutes before your presentation:
   • walk into the room acting more confident than you feel.
   • every time a little excitement surfaces, remember the first words to your Opening and silently repeat them every chance you get.
   • a little anticipation excitement is normal - and good! Remember the first time you kissed someone? You're less anxious now but you're thinking of it in a less positive light.

6. Just before you speak:
   • slowly scan audience for a full two seconds as you relax your shoulders, smile, and take a deep breath. Speak louder than you think you should.

7. Post presentation analysis:
   • compare your anxiety today to other presentations; determine for yourself why it was so much less.
   • calculate time it took to run through simple exercises and subtract time you would have used blabbing about presentation fear.
   • know that it gets easier and easier!
   • imagine the opportunities in your career and your life when you can present without fear!
   • mentally accept the congratulations of your author. Good Job!

Warning: Too much?

It's not uncommon for some of my compulsive presenters to employ this strategy so obsessively, that they become completely relaxed and then present in a (let's say) uninspired manner. They find it difficult to become the least bit energized during their presentations. In effect, the strategy has worked too well for them.

If this happens to you, recognize how significantly you've changed your irrational presentation thoughts and then get about the business of making dynamic presentations. You have a responsibility to be enthused about your presentation material for your audience members. And now that you have some time before your next presentation that you don't have to spend being afraid, why not focus on turning a great presentation into an outstanding one?

STEP 9
REHEARSE OUT LOUD.

If you walked to the edge of a diving board about 20-feet above a swimming pool and slipped off, you'd fall into the pool, right? One hopes that your honesty, your mortality, and the laws of science guarantee a positive response.

Now let's change the scenario just a bit. Let's put you back up on that board in a little skimpy bathing suit, fill the stands with your superiors and peers from work (all expecting you to do pretty well), and seat five judges with scorecards in hand looking expectantly in your direction.

Now - let's see a dive!

What's that you say? You can't dive? Of course you can dive! Get back on that board, Boscoe. If you can fall into the water, you can dive into the water! Right?

You're nervous? Nervous about what? Well, doesn't matter; here's a fine trick all great divers use: imagine your judges are naked! That's a corker, heh? Whadaya mean you're nervous because you don't know exactly how to do it? What a baby! None of us knows how do to it - we can dive into the water because we can fall into the water - that's all.

Tell you what we'll do; we'll give you a diving visual aid. It's a big piece of distorted glass placed between the pool and the spectators that makes you look sleeker and faster and eliminates your flailing arms and legs. By the time the crowd tries to figure out what it's seeing in the glass, you're already in the water! Great, heh?

What? Maybe you'd like some diving lessons? Ohhh, brother. All right, all right. Here's a book teaching you how to dive. As soon as you finish reading it, get back on that board, the judges are waiting.

As you've probably guessed, I'm using this strange diving episode as an analogy to most presenters today. People wrongly assume, if you can speak, you can present and push you out to be judged with few skills, some bewildering "aids," some worthless ruses, and a total lack of rehearsal. Is it any wonder you slither into the pool like a reticent reptile or smack the surface in a loud belly flop?

By the time you've reached this point in the book, you've been exposed to over ten dozen (!) solid presentation ideas. (See "A Quick Reference Guide to 175 Presentation Ideas in this Book," page 195. I'll also deliver a few dozen more before we're finished.) I hope you're impressed with this intellectual smorgasbord of ways to help yourself become a great presenter. But here's a simple statement with which you should be equally impressed:

> not one of these ideas can help you if
> you don't rehearse out loud.

You may have wondered why I attempted to get you rehearsing out loud as early as Step 2 in my formula. The reason is simple. Rehearsing out loud is not something you tack on to the end of your presentation if you have the time; it's an integral part of creating it. Since a presentation is meant to be spoken out loud, speaking the different elements of its composition as you think of them is the only natural and intelligent thing to do.

"Think before you speak," is a wonderful cliche for most facets of life. But "speak to yourself out loud as you think," is much more appropriate for presentations. After you've created your message while rehearsing it out loud, you must then rehearse out loud again to revise and rejuvenate it. If you find in this book the word 'rehearsal' not immediately followed by 'out loud,' you may assume it is an error. Rehearsals are never in your mind, they're always in your mouth.

What's the best way to rehearse?

Let's start by defining rehearsal in a practical way for presenters. Rehearsal is the process by which you become very comfortable with the objective, structure, and key points of your message and the verbal manner in which you'll deliver those elements to your audience.

I think of positive presentation rehearsal as a procedure that goes on at three distinct levels: the creation level, the review level, and the pre-audience audience level.

The creation level of rehearsal. This level is perhaps best exemplified in Step 2, when you say your objective out loud a number of times. Writing the objective on a page and actually saying it are two very different things. Although an objective may "work," on paper, if you can't say it clearly and distinctively, it's not right for a presentation. The same is true for numbered key points and openings and closings.

The review level of rehearsal. After creating your objective, your numbered key points and your opening and closing, this level comes into play. How smoothly do these elements slide together out loud? When you add your preview · go through · review structure, does it sound right to you? Can you say it easily out loud without notes? Can you think it through on your feet because it follows so logically and is so well-structured?

The pre-audience audience level of rehearsal. As good as your presentation may now sound to you, it should be tested on someone else's ears. Others such as peers, spouses, friends, and family, should hear the basic structure at least once (opening, objective, preview, go through, review, closing) before your real audience does.

Doesn't all of this take a lot of time?

It undoubtedly takes more time than you're spending now, but consider the presentations you're delivering now.

As a general rule, you should plan to spend a minimum of one hour rehearsal time for any presentation, and two hours (or more) for any presentation over ten or fifteen minutes. You'll notice that even in the extreme example of my formula, when presenters only have two hours to deliver a great presentation, I recommend 25 percent of that time be devoted to the second level of rehearsals alone. In the formula, they are also rehearsing out loud while they create their presentations.

I just don't have that kind of time!

Sorry - if you don't have the time to rehearse out loud, you don't have time to be a good presenter - it's that simple. I wish I could make it easier for you. I wish I could devise some formula or invent some technique that would eliminate the need to rehearse out loud but I can't. No one can.

I've simplified to a great degree the time you spend creating presentations, utilizing visual aids, highlighting key points, cutting details, eliminating dull verbosity, choosing great openings and closings, and even a time-saving way to truly reduce presentation anxiety. But I cannot conjure up any slick trick that will significantly reduce the time you spend coordinating the wonderful structured ideas in your mind with the words that come out of your mouth. To my mind, none exists.

In fact, if one existed and I knew about it, I don't know if I would be doing you a favor by teaching it to you.

Why?

There must be some cost to becoming a great presenter. There may not be much of a price in delivering one great presentation (except for learning my formula) but there is a cost in becoming a great presenter. If it came in a bottle and was available to everyone, everyone would be a great presenter and, of course, no one would be because the standards would skyrocket.

When I hear people say they want to become great presenters but don't have the time, I'm reminded of a lot of 'wannabe's' whose main efforts towards their goals seem to be telling people like me what they want to be.

"I wanna be rich."
"I wanna be smart."
"I wanna be independent."
"I wanna be in a job like yours!"

While all these goals are fine, surely these people must have learned after the age of three that nothin' comes for nothin' - there's always a cost! Time and time again I run into people who tell me they don't have time to rehearse even one hour for important presentations. Within a few hours over lunch they're also telling me what great jobs they have because they were able to get to the golf course two or three times that week or how they spent three hours over some exotic dinner the evening before.

I'm not criticizing golf or exotic dinners or the people who enjoy them, I'm merely saying if you want to be a great presenter - with all of the prestige and reward that entails - you must be willing to sacrifice the time it takes to rehearse out loud. There's no other way.

Why do you recommend that I speak twice as loud as I normally do when I rehearse out loud and present?

I'm glad you've read this far. You're about to learn one of the most important secrets of rehearsing out loud and delivering your presentations in a commanding way:

> a strong, compelling voice is often the most
> significant factor that determines who is
> a great presenter and who is a common one.

Audiences are mesmerized by powerful voices. They attribute qualities to these that go beyond the scope of reason. They interpret presenters who have compelling voices as confident, in-charge, action-oriented, dynamic, intelligent, and just about every other adjective by which one would ideally choose to be described.

Most people have a superficial idea about projection in presentations. They think you project to be heard by all audience members. Although speaking to be heard is the most basic job of presentation projection, it's roughly equivalent to dining out in the most elegant restaurant in town so you won't go hungry. Certainly there are many other and better reasons to dine at that establishment than stopping hunger pangs. Think of the ambiance, the experience of the special occasion, the adventure of creative cuisine, and the wonderful memory. If you just want to chow down - go to Bill's Hots!

I always forcefully make this point to my seminar people by using my own voice projection as an example. After speaking for about ten minutes in my "presentation voice" during the first module, I arrive at this section on the importance of projection. Immediately I lower my volume by about one half or two thirds and direct my remarks to the person seated furthest from me.

"Presentation projection involves much more than 'hearing the words,' doesn't it?" I'll quietly say to that audience member, "I'm fairly sure you can hear every word I'm saying now, can't you?"

Audience reaction at this moment is one of complete surprise. When I switch from a presentational to a conversational level of speaking, their reaction is always immediate and always negative. I'm no longer the presenter I've established in their minds.

"All right," I'll quietly continue, "what's different about the way I'm now speaking?"

The comments are nearly always the same,

"There's no life to your voice."

"You don't sound as sincere or committed."

"What you're saying doesn't sound important."

"Now it's just like you're talking."

A proper projection level does a number of great things for presentations:

- It adds life to your voice.

Years ago I discovered a louder presentation voice destroyed the bugaboo of many bland presenters: the monotone. When presenters were projecting properly, they naturally seemed to "punch" (emphasize) certain words and take longer, more appropriate pauses (probably for breath). This vocal variance greatly enhanced their delivery and required virtually no effort on their parts except for the increase in volume.

- It makes what you say sound more important.

Often when people talk in conversations, they babble. I don't mean to criticize here (and I'm sure I'm as guilty as the next person) but if you cut from most peoples' conversations idle chatter, gossip, weather talk, symptom and illness rundowns, and sports talk - you wouldn't have much left. To distinguish your presentation from the normal plethora of prattle, you must make it sound different. Turning up your volume is the fastest way to do that.

- It makes you sound more committed.

How can you tell if someone is really committed to something about which he is talking? Three ways: a faster rate of speech, a larger display of animation including gestures, and greater volume. Audience members want presenters committed to their presentations. Before those members buy on to new ideas, they've got to be sure the person advocating those ideas is even more committed than he asks them to be. Greater vocal volume is almost universally accepted as greater commitment.

• It makes you sound more confident.

There are some common phrases that are especially relevant to this point. Think of "quietly confident," or "confident in a quiet way." The point here is that confidence is so closely associated with loud or powerful voices, when a confident impression is given in a quiet manner, descriptive words are added to explain the apparent dichotomy to the reader or listener.

For much of our culture, loudness translates into confidence. This is too bad for most presenters (who become nervous and subsequently quieter in presentations) but it is especially unfortunate for women presenters.

Especially unfortunate for women?

Yes. Quietness has always been taught as a feminine 'plus' in our culture and most women I coach have a difficult time raising their voices to demonstrate authority. Some find it physically uncomfortable, others believe it makes them sound angry. However, since many women I coach are used to working harder than most men, once the effectiveness of greater vocal volume is demonstrated to them, they work harder to achieve it and often do extremely well.

That isn't fair.

I agree. But wait - it gets worse! In addition to confidence and authority being established by greater vocal volume to most audiences, they're also demonstrated by lower vocal tone. This is certainly harder for many women to achieve. So in addition to presenting louder, they must also present lower in tone than they're used to speaking.

Present louder and lower than men?

No, present louder and lower than they normally do. Once again, although it is initially harder for women to achieve this in presentations, once they do, they often become outstanding presenters.

Are you saying women generally are better presenters than men?

I'm saying for anyone to become a great presenter, she or he must recognize both the rewards and the costs involved. In business, the rewards are faster career advancement and greater recognition by senior management. These costs involve learning new skills, taking risks, putting yourself into situations which may initially be uncomfortable, and putting more time into the effort (i.e. rehearsing longer). It seems to me, women have recognized these presentation opportunities better than men and are more willing to work harder to achieve them.

What about tape or video recorders for rehearsal?

Excellent idea. Tape recorders are especially good at the second level of rehearsal, the 'review' level. Put the recorder five or ten feet from you and project your opening, objective, key points and closing a few times. When you play it back, try to objectively imagine yourself in your audiences' seat. What did you like about the structure and flow? What needs to be changed?

Video recorders are best for the 'pre-audience audience' rehearsal. Listen to the comments and then run back the tape to determine if you can see what the pre-audience member saw.

During my rehearsals, I keep changing the words I use when I try to explain my points.

Great! That's what's supposed to happen. Your mouth and your brain are trying different combinations to see which ones make more sense and are easier to deliver and explain. Keep rehearsing. During your presentation the "right" combination often seems to pop up most times if you've rehearsed adequately.

Remember now, we're not trying to memorize your presentation. (Danger! See page 89 immediately!) What we're doing is familiarizing yourself enough with the structure of your presentation to easily talk through your points.

I'm still having difficulty determining how loudly I should project.

I'm not surprised, most people do at first. Remember the first few times you heard yourself on a tape recorder? It didn't sound like you, did it? The reason is that when you hear yourself most times, you're actually listening from the outside plus you're listening to the sounds from inside your head. The sound waves and vibrations are bouncing around bones and reverberating throughout cavities (sinus, not dental) so the voice you hear is louder and fuller. Of course, there are no such enhancers on recording devices or on the ears of your audience.

To compensate for the audio discrepancy between you and your audience members,

• address your remarks initially to the people sitting furthest from you and,

• speak louder than you think you should and sometimes even (to you) inappropriately loud!

It's best to try out this last one in your final rehearsal with a pre-audience audience but you'll still be surprised. While you think you're shouting, they'll be admiring your strong confident, committed tones. Ask them!

Isn't there a chance I can over-rehearse and go stale?

Your chances of getting hit by a meteorite are better.

If you've become so familiar with your presentation material and are getting bored with it, remember your responsibility to your audience concerning enthusiasm and my neighbor's piano-pounding kid.

Take those well-worn words and DO something with them! Boost your volume even more! Watch one of those old time preachers on television and see if you can mimic their delivery with your material! Have a little fun. Start your presentation in the middle and see if you can follow it through the beginning right to the place where you started. If you can, you know you have the structure down, now DO something with the words.

I like to rehearse silently at my desk going over my notes. Isn't this a rehearsal?

It sure is - it's a rehearsal for delivering silent presentations at your desk. Now if there's ever a big need for that type of presentation, you're the first person they should trot out. But for real presentations, you must rehearse out loud - there's just no other way.

Summary

Rehearsing out loud is probably the most important thing you can do to deliver a great presentation. As you probably noticed, I tried to motivate you to rehearse out loud in my formula as early as possible - as early as your objective in Step 2. Rehearsing out loud is not something you tack on to a presentation - it is an integral part of creating it. If you don't have time for adequate rehearsal, you don't have time to become a great presenter - it's that definite.

I think of rehearsal in three distinct levels:

1. The Creation Level: when you speak different presentation components as you create them.

2. The Review Level: when you've created the major components of your presentation (opening, objective, preview, go-through, review, and closing) and speak these to see how they flow and sound. Tape recorders are good aids here. And,

3. The Pre-audience Audience Level: when you test your presentation on a "trial" audience composed of peers or friends. A video camera is valuable at this level to see if you can recognize your audience's comments about you and your style on screen during playback.

A presentation rehearsal out loud also gives you the opportunity to learn how to project properly. This is vital for a great presentation.

Presentations without proper rehearsals are the awful equivalent of "rehearsing in public." Your audience deserves much more.

Section 3

MISCELLANEOUS

HOW WILL YOUR AUDIENCE JUDGE YOU?

We know the actual beginning of your presentation starts when one audience member begins to form an impression about you. This impression will influence how he feels about your presentation. We also know that a large percentage of an audience's perception of a presentation is not based on the actual presentation - it's based on the presenter. How you "come across" as a presenter, largely determines how successful your presentation will be.

What's the basis for an audience's judgment on a a presenter? Here are some of the highlights of that judgment and what you can do to control them in your favor:

1. By your prepresentation impression.

Few presentations begin with a blank slate. Most of the time, audience members will have an idea of the professionalism, credibility, and likability of a presenter. If they don't know or haven't heard about a particular presenter, this perception may be formed by written material, knowledge of the presenter's company or family, or even stereotyping in regard to attributes such as race, age, and sex. (Audiences definitely do not comply with Federal regulations regarding discrimination!)

What you do:

Act as professionally and as competently as possible. Return telephone calls promptly. Arrive early. Be assertive without being a pain concerning your presentation needs.

Have your introduction written and ready to deliver that day. Go over it with the person who will introduce you.

(Hint: if it's possible without seeming discourteous, avoid contact with audience members before your presentation. I would much rather have them make a first impression of you based on that well-rehearsed opening, rather than on inane chit-chat.)

2. By your audience contact.

The ideal presentation style is a pleasing balance between professionalism and humanness. Audience members must feel you're competent and knowledgeable and they must also feel you're an actual human being to whom they can relate. Good salespeople know a customer must buy the seller before he buys the product or service. Good presenters should know the same thing in regard to their audience members.

What you do:

Good presenters make contact with audience members in three essential ways: eye contact, voice contact, and body contact. Eye contact is equally important to voice contact. The general rule is every audience member should feel you are making eye contact with him at least part of the time in your presentation. Each time you look away, you give that member a chance to intellectually "check out" of your talk. The more you can avoid notes (rehearse!) the more eye contact you can make and the better off you will be in the presentation.

If you have an extremely difficult time with eye contact, first, recognize just how important it is; second, use the anxiety-reducing strategy beginning on page 139 to feel better about it, and third, if it's still a a problem, look at peoples' eyebrows. No one will be able to tell even from a few feet (and I sure won't tell).

Establish audience contact by getting out from behind that podium and stop hiding behind notes, visual aids, and technical jargon. Your goal is to establish a human bond with your audience. Become a presence; cut as much distance as you reasonably can between you and audience members. This is especially true if your physical stature is not overwhelming. On a stage or platform, don't stand near "reference points" of podiums or people. Help your audience measure you in terms of effect as opposed to inches.

3. By your energy and enthusiasm.

We've talked about this before but it cannot be emphasized too much. Audience members expect the presenter to be enthused and committed to his ideas before they're willing to endorse them. Energy and enthusiasm, of course, must be demonstrated in proper ways. If a presenter is overbearing in his exuberance and boundless in his fervor, credibility is destroyed. Well over nine out of ten presenters don't have to worry about going overboard, however. Most look and act as bored as most audience members.

What you do:

Think of how people speak when they're excited: they talk faster and louder than they usually do. They're much more animated and they frequently smile more than normally. All you do is take those traits, turn up the volume on them for presentations, and present yourself and your ideas to audience members in a positively excited manner.

4. By your authority over the presentation environment.

Audiences like 'take-charge' presenters. They respond well to presenters who are in command of the entire presentation environment including the words, the sights, the sounds, and the feelings. If these presenters do not abuse an audience's trust, they are quickly known as outstanding presenters - rare gems in the rocky world of words.

What you do:

Take charge.As presenter, you're in charge of every aspect of your presentation situation. This includes a total command of your material without the extensive use of distracting notes, all the visual aids, the possible interruptions, the lights and temperature, the seating, and even the prepresentation knowledge level of audience members. Obviously, if you're seeing your presentation environment and hearing your presentation for the first time along with your audience members - neither of you will like what you see and hear. Extensive rehearsal and preplanning is the only sane way to go.

5. By delivering a Great Presentation.

Here's where a great presenter and presentation reinforce each other in the audience member's mind. An audience member bases a large part of his perception of a presentation on the presenter himself. If the presenter is delivering a strong, clear, well-structured message, the audience member often assumes he's a good presenter. Since he's a good presenter, the audience member further assumes he's delivering a good presentation! As a matter of fact, he's right!

What you do:

Simple, deliver a great presentation. You're holding a book that teaches you how - now do it!

Your audience member is seated; he's looking to you for a presentation. If you do your best to control his initial perception in a professional way, establish eye, voice, and body contact with him, demonstrate some energy and enthusiasm, take charge of every aspect of the presentation environment, and deliver a great presentation in a memorable way, you may be the best presenter this audience member has heard in his entire life. Be assured, he will never forget you.

DUMB ADVICE ON PRESENTATIONS

Throughout this book, you've read why the presentation situation is so appalling today. People wrongly think "if you can talk, you can present," and then don't teach you basic, practical skills and give you enough opportunities to practice those skills to feel comfortable before an audience. That's the main reason most presentations are awful. But there's another reason that's just as despicable: dumb advice.

Presentation dumb advice comes from a lot of sources. Dumb advice comes from people who can make good presentations and those who can't. It comes from people who should know better and those who don't. Some of it comes from years of antiquated tradition (such as complete memorization); some from modern inventions (laser pointers!)

Perhaps the worse dumb advice comes from generalization. One presenter on one occasion hits a lucky fluke and thinks he's discovered THE WAY. Let's take the case of Joe Blow. Joe shows up at meeting one day totally unprepared to make a presentation but circumstances force him to speak. He stands up in utter terror and blurts out whatever pops into his mind. Since he's not prepared, he doesn't speak as long as he normally would and his fear actually makes him sound more committed.

His audience members respond positively. They weren't expecting much in the first place because they've heard Joe speak before and would only recommend the experience to people who have trouble sleeping. Since their expectations were dismal and Joe certainly exceeded them, they congratulate him on a good presentation.

"Whoa!" thinks Blow, "That's the secret! Don't prepare

- just speak from the heart and the audience thinks I'm Winston Churchill! Since I prepared so much in the past and put people to sleep, this must be the way to really wow 'em!"

Of course word of Joe's "great presentation" travels quickly throughout the village. The natives embellish it a little with each telling and by the time Fred Schmoe hears the story, there were tears in the audience's eyes and they gave Joe a standing ovation. And when it's Schmoe's turn to make a presentation, to whom does he turn?

"Joe," he says, "I heard you made an awesome, inspiring, heart-wrenching speech at that meeting last week! I have to speak next. How did you do it?"

So Joe, once a yawn-inspiring droner, now a presentation inspiration, looks at the student at his feet and says with the authority of ageless wisdom, "Don't prepare a thing, friend, speak to the audience from your heart - they'll feel the message."

"Wow!" thinks Schmoe, "that's the secret. And it's so easy!"

I'm sure you know the rest. I'll spare you the ugly details of the audience's looks of pity and disgust as Fred, trying to remember some obscure point, launches into a bizarre story of Larry the Lizard, his seventh grade best friend. It was not a pretty sight.

Fred was the victim of Presentation Dumb Advice. Don't you be! Regardless of the source, regardless of the circumstances, if anyone gives you any of the following gems of dumb advice - run! That's right, run! Don't explain. Don't be polite. Just run!

"Rehearse in front of a mirror."

Years ago I heard the same thing you probably heard about how to rehearse presentations. "Stand in front of a mirror," teachers used to tell me, "and watch yourself as you speak." I've been in the presentation business now for over

20 and I still don't know what the hell they were talking about!

People simply can't think about two different things at the same time. You can't watch yourself in a mirror to see how you're coming across and still concentrate on what you're saying. It's the intellectual equivalent of rubbing your stomach with one hand and patting your head with the other except it's about one thousand times harder.

Now it's bad enough that this dumb advice is generously passed out. What's worse is that when these brilliant ideas don't work for people, they have a tendency to throw up their hands and say, "I'll never be a good presenter, I can't watch myself in the mirror and think at the same time!" What they should say is, "What idiot thought this was a good idea in the first place?"

"Imagine your audience naked."

As a professional speaker, I can tell you I can't think of anything more distracting to serious communication than imagining an entire room full of naked people sitting in front of you listening. It's a terribly diverting thought if the audience members are all attractive and it's just a terrible thought if they're not. Although the idea gives new impact to the term audience "members," it's hardly the thing that will relax you (it's stated intent).

If I was to advocate inflexible rules regarding the reduction of presentation anxiety, the first would certainly be, "no nudes is good nudes."

"Wing it."

"Winging it" is for the birds. Remember the story of Joe Blow and Fred Schmoe? That's about how it usually goes based on my experience. Just because a presenter tells you he's "winging it," doesn't necessarily make it so. And often people who were not even in the actual presentation are telling you about great wingers - and they heard it from someone else.

Once I coached an upcoming top executive in a company who got himself into more of a fine mess than I could get him out of. He was to deliver a brief eight to ten-minute message via videotape to his hundreds of salespeople across the country. He wanted to speak out of doors in a remote location (which was fine), in a relaxed manner (which was fine), straight from his heart without notes and without a plan (which is fine only if you have lips on your aorta and nothing to say).

I asked one of his aids to have the video production company bring a camera teleprompter to make life easier for everyone. Uh-uh; seems Mr. "Wing" had convinced everyone that he always spoke from the heart and didn't need notes or a teleprompter. In fact, the expensive production company should only be hired for one hour because he was sure to do it in one take. Right.

Scene 1: 1:30 p.m. Beautiful sunshine; expensive, professional production company set to shoot; Mr. "Wing" looking confident. Director signals camera man and points to Mr. "Wing." Five seconds, six seconds pass. Finally "Wing" says, "Can we start this again? I thought you were going to say action."

Scene 2: 5:45 p.m. We stopped counting the "takes" after the fifteenth or sixteenth. There are about four of us now on our hands and knees furiously trying to write a script on cue cards which we fashioned from torn up cardboard boxes. We're getting scared because our box supply is dwindling; we had to rip up some earlier "just as notes," but "Wing" couldn't speak from those either. Every minute the overtime charges on the production crew are racing towards the national debt but it no longer matters - the sun is setting.

"Is it always this complicated?" chuckles "Wing."
Wing it?   Please don't.

"Have a few belts."

I was to speak after dinner at a convention in Chicago.
Since the waiters were serving dessert and pouring coffee, I
knew I had about ten minutes or so before my presentation.
I excused myself from my dinner guests and watched as one
of my hosts, seated a few places down, did the same thing.
I thought nothing of it, proceeded to the rest room and so
did he. When my "shadow's" bathroom duties seemed to
consist of little but watching me in the mirror, I probably
appeared a little apprehensive.

"I'm sorry, Mr. Paolo," he explained, "but we had quite
an experience with our last dinner speaker. He snuck into the
mens' room, got completely bombed, and then babbled like
an idiot for his whole presentation. We even refused to pay
him! The chairman asked me to kind of keep an eye on you."

I laughed with relief. "No problem," I said, "I usually
don't make it a habit to get bombed in strange mens' rooms
and I won't make an exception tonight."

Alcohol and public speakers. Although the two have been
linked together for years, it's really an unfortunate marriage.
At first it might not seem that way. After all, why should
a speaker be dull and wimpy, when, for the price of a few
drinks, he can be eloquent and powerful?

But it just doesn't work out like that. Alcohol rarely
helps presenters. I don't mean it turns them into raving
drunks who slur their words and insult their audiences (although this sometimes happens), what it usually does is "slips
them out of focus." In other words, it dulls them; they're
not as sharp, or as bright, or as able to respond to instant
problems and opportunities in the midst of a presentation.
Worse, presenters lose the ability to measure their effectiveness both in the presentation and when it's over.

One other problem with alcohol is that although it may relax you somewhat during your presentation, you still haven't decided to understand what makes you nervous in the first place - and what you can do about it naturally and consistently. A fine bottle of wine or a few drinks seem like a reasonable reward to yourself for delivering an outstanding presentation on which you worked very hard and took some risks. But before you speak? Dumb advice.

"Read a script."

There are only three things wrong with scripted presentations: 1. someone's got to write it, 2. you're got to read it, and 3. your audience has got to listen to it.

Writing a presentation is a highly skilled discipline. The spoken word is quite different from the written word; a fact that seems to escape most people who write their own presentations. Unless you have the luxury of a professional speechwriter (about $80 - $100 per completed script minute; i.e. $1600 - $2000 for a 20-minute speech), you're going to have to write it yourself.

Even though you may have won third place in the Daughters of the American Revolution's Patriotism Essay Contest in the ninth grade, you may now have difficulty writing a cohesive note to your newspaper boy when you leave for vacation. Speech writing is not easy.

Nor is speech reading. That's also a highly skilled art. It takes as much knowledge, experience, and rehearsal to read a speech well as it does to deliver a less programmed presentation.

But let's say you can get a satisfactory speech written and you'll rehearse it enough times to be reasonably comfortable with it. Are there any other problems?

Just one: your audience has to listen to it.

When we were kids, it was fun being read to. It was

fun right up until the time we were three or four years old and started to learn how to read. Then it wasn't that much fun anymore. We didn't just want to sit back and listen - we wanted to read ourselves! Audiences still do.

There's a tremendous presentation cost in a completely written script. The terrible price includes most eye contact, a solid rapport with audience members in the first few minutes, a restriction on natural movement and gestures, a toll on flexibility in words and tone, spontaneity, naturalness, and general audience respect (after all, most people can read, few can present in a compelling way).

Read a script? Only to audiences of two-year olds who can't read it themselves.

"Just make your presentation as informal as possible."

"Hey, take your coat off, have a seat, roll up your sleeves, tell a few jokes - what the hell? You're among friends here. Don't bother with anything planned, just talk to us."

Oh, what a tempting tar pool this is to inexperienced presenters. After all, we should please the audience right? If they want "laid back," we should give 'em "laid back," right? If they want to hear it a certain way, that's the way we deliver it right? Wrong. Get away from that tar pool!

Audience members tell presenters all sorts of things. So do gamblers named "Doc" and the guys on the sidewalk who want to teach you new card games on cardboard boxes.

If you've done even one quarter of the preparation necessary for a great presentation, you know what's best to achieve your objective. It undoubtedly includes a healthy dose of professionalism that demands you stand up, roll down and button your sleeves, put on and button your suit jacket (by the way, I'm not being sexist here - women rarely fall for the old "be less than a professional" line - they know what it costs in credibility) and act like somebody. Somebody you're audience can respect and trust and believe. You can still be "one of the boys" later - the very second after you achieve your presentation objective.

"Pace back and forth to give the audience something to watch and to relieve your anxiety."

Are you a gerbil on a wheel? Do you need exercise? Is your audience so visually deprived, they're actually stimulated by watching you pace back and forth with no apparent destination as the energy you need for a powerful presentation drains all over the floor in pointless little quick steps?

What's going on here?

The first time I ever heard that anyone had given one of my people this recommendation, I laughed out loud. I really thought someone was kidding or the presenter got the advice wrong. The next thousand or two times I heard it, it wasn't so funny. It seems to be common advice.

Now friends, let's think rationally about this. Remember the necessity of eye contact and voice contact? Are you pacing like I assume you're pacing or are you sidestepping to retain audience contact? (This must certainly provide some fascinating visual stimulation.) Are you focusing your audience's attention on your face - your most compelling non-verbal communicator - or on your moving ears and your little dancing feet?

But the ultimate lunacy here is someone gave you this moronic advice and you probably didn't burst out laughing or take a swing at the piker did you? At least now you'll know what to do next time.

"Use lots of quotations."

"I do not choose to quote." — Fred the "expert mechanic" who used to pretend to fix my car, when asked for an estimate, on July 7, 1987.

I don't mean to disillusion you or anything, (God knows) but do you want me to tell you what most quotations really are - besides cliches? Until the advent of radio and television, they were what some dead guy either heard, or thought he heard, or was supposed to have heard, or wanted to hear, from another dead guy and then he wrote it down as he remembered it, or wanted to remember it, or how he wanted us to remember it.

Most respectable sources list many quotations as "apocryphal," or, "we doubt if this person really said these words, but it sounds like something he'd say." Right.

"Apocryphal" covers about 5000 years of quotation history. Now for the last eighty or ninety years, since the electronic media plugged in, two significant quotation trends have emerged.

First, there aren't nearly as many rich, relevant words of wisdom as there used to be because no one today has the moxie to embellish them as they did before tangible records existed.[1] Second, the few that are quotable ("Ask not . . . ," "I have a dream . . .") have been pounded into our ears so many times, schoolchildren must wonder if our leaders suffer from some type of oratorical aphasia mumbling the same

---

[1] There's one striking exception that redefines moxie: Neil Armstrong's "one small step" moon quotation. When you stop to think about it, "one small step for man, one giant leap for mankind," makes very little sense. It seems in the excitement of the moment, Mr. Armstrong forgot to say the word "a" in front of the word "man." Now this is perfectly understandable - presenters have certainly become flustered by far less. But without its modifier "a," "man" means pretty much the same thing as "mankind" and renders the quote meaningless. Not to worry. In the best centuries-old tradition of quotation manipulation, many sources now list "This is one small step for a man . . ." as what Armstrong actually said. Among the sources: *Encyclopedia Britannica* and Bartlett's *Familiar Quotations*.

few words again and again. This mindless parroting not only does a disservice to some great people, it's enough to jettison virtually any presentation into the seamy depths of triteness.

Yet presenters still believe that dusty old quotes will add life to their talks.

A true story. When I first started to write speeches for corporate executives, one of my first assignments was with an ornery old coot who still believed in corporate America - as it was in about 1910 or '20. I was ushered into his plush office high in the tower by an overly efficient secretary who had had her blood replaced by antifreeze. He was on the telephone and pointed to a chair in which I sat. He said about 20 words to me which he wanted turned into 2000 words in exactly two days.

When I returned in 48 hours, I handed him the script, sat in my little chair, and waited as he began to read it to himself. When he came to a choice selection of (if I may immodestly say) some rather well-executed phrases, he looked at me and said, "Who said this?"

I didn't understand. I immediately thought to myself, "Is this a trick question? The rules for ghostwriting are pretty clear: I say the words, you send me a check, then, you can say the words - isn't that how it works?"

Seeing the puzzled look on my face, he spoke again, "I mean from whom did you quote these phrases? They're rather good but I need to give the source."

"Oh," I said, too dumb to know where this was leading, "I thought of those; I didn't quote anyone."

"Oh," he said surprised, clearly disappointed, and now mildly annoyed, "Well, I can't quote you." ('You smarmy little twit' was implied but not stated as he ignored the fact that he was quoting me every single word of his speech.) "See if you can find some similar words by someone famous."

I calculated the chance of me actually finding "similar words by someone famous" in the next 24 hours as roughly about one in one thousand. Further, I calculated the chances of me actually looking for these words and then substituting them for my own at roughly one in ten million.

I mean, why would I kill myself to substitute somebody elses' words (which probably weren't really his in the first place) for mine - so this guy could substitute (what were claimed to be) the first guy's words for his (which were really mine anyway)? It made no sense to me, so I did what I've done on a number of similar occasions, I turned to someone wiser: Thomas Alva Edison.

In corporate America, there's no more oft-quoted font of wisdom than this brilliant inventor. But let me tell you a little secret about Mr. Edison: if Thomas Edison really said all the things corporate speechwriters have said he's said, the little motormouth wouldn't have had the time to invent anything! Whenever we get in a bind, lucky Mr. Edison is the first one we trot out with another quote.

You see, Edison had three great things going for him: first, he was a genius; second, he was a champion of what made corporate America great: the Protestant work ethic; and third, there are only a very few, barely audible, scratchy recordings of him actually saying anything at all. The rest was told to us by various other people - the same way quotes were attributed to Socrates and his ilk thousands of years ago. How perfect!

So although Edison may have said, "Genius is one percent inspiration and ninety-nine percent perspiration," so could have Ming Lao in 2256 B.C., Edison's publicist long after the inventor died, or your Uncle Harry at a drunken family reunion in '57. So who cares?

My client cared. When I brought him my newly shuffled words and attributed them to Thomas Edison, he looked pleased. In fact, he looked downright misty-eyed for a moment. His Universe was right again.

Don't do this to your audiences. They've come to hear your ideas; your view of the world - don't deny that to them. The world has never experienced (nor ever will) another person who is exactly like you - give us the chance!

And don't you dare quote me on this!

"Put a finger to your thumb and squeeze to relieve anxiety during a presentation."

I know I'm going to get into trouble here. If you do this now and it works for you, just get to the next section - fast! Forget I'm even questioning the method. Of course, if it does work for you, and you also have some money to invest in a guaranteed land deal, please call my office as soon as possible. We'll work something out.

For the rest of you hardened cynics, let me tell you about the newest presentation anxiety-reducing technique, the finger-thumb squeeze. It's so "new age," you will actually hear the clinking of crystals just as Shirley as your bad presentation vibes will center themselves and then dissipate into space.

Of course the finger-thumb squeeze is only one digit removed from the combination you use when you snap your fingers (same thumb, one finger over). And here's another hot flash for you - they both work equally well, if you believe they will!

I am not against all placebos; I think the medical community did itself a grave disservice when it banned them decades ago. In fact, they really only banned "sugar pill" placebos; today you can still buy many placebos from your drug store shelves. The difference is they come in neat packages and cost you a lot more money but at least the advertisements still speak highly of them.

Anyway, placebos in presentations are risky. Although their users don't really know why they work, this isn't too bad - as long as they continue to work. The problem occurs on that inevitable day when they don't. You see, back-up plans for placebos are taboo. Anything that even implies they might not work is dangerous because it shakes the crumbly base upon which the belief is created.

So if you're in front of an audience and are thrown by an impolite question, and you squeeze your thumb and finger together and nothing happens, then what? Then part of your mind races around trying to figure out what went wrong, as another part races around trying to find the answer to the question, as another part tries to dam the rushing flood of panic with no available tools. By the time you get all this straightened out, your audience will have walked out shaking their heads and clucking like the 60-Minutes ticker.

Remember the guy who walked around New York City snapping his fingers to keep elephants away? ("See, it works!") What they didn't tell you is they also found an elephant gun in his apartment! He might have been bonkerss but at least he had a backup plan.

"Don't buy *Make a Great Presentation in Two Hours!*, I'll lend you my copy."

Truly the dumbest advice of all.

EXCUSES

So many times in my seminars, I drag people to great presentations while they're kicking and screaming and cursing. I beg them, I implore them, I beseech them - to attempt the things I ask. There's not a new excuse you could give me for not trying my methods - I've heard 3000 of them! Try to imagine a continual, whining stream of screeching voices bleating:

- "I'm not comfortable doing it that way!"
- "We don't do it that way!"
- "That won't work for me!"
- "That won't work with my audiences."
- "I tried that once before!"
- "I tried that once and somebody laughed at me!"
- "I tried that once and I couldn't stop laughing!"
- "I feel like an idiot!"
- "Are you trying to make an actor out of me?"
- "If I don't feel it, I can't express it!"
- "Louder?"
- "I don't talk like that!"
- "Louder than this!?"
- "You're kidding!"
- "I'm too tired/confused/overwhelmed/overworked!"
- "I don't feel well!"
- "You do it first!"
- "Would you do that again? I'll pay attention this time!"
- "I can't do that! (Pause) Nope, can't do that either!"
- (Bellowing) "I can't speak louder than that! (realizing that she just did). Well, I can't always speak that loud!"
- "Well, I'll try it but I won't like it."

There are two reasons my seminars don't turn into bloody brawls at times (three if you count the fact I wouldn't be paid or get invitations to return). The first is the feedback from other seminar participants (usually peers of the complainers) and the second is the camcorder.

After the excuse-ridden, reluctant presenter tries out a few of the horrible, disfiguring techniques I've suggested in front of the class (often only as a "favor" to me, not because he believes they'll work) his peers usually give him such positive feedback, he's amazed.

- "I've never seen Joe present like that before."
- "Joe, you looked really confident and in-charge!"
- "I've seen Joe present for three years but never this good!"
- "He appears so authoritative - so comfortable - so, well, unlike himself!"

Joe, of course, doesn't believe it.

"C'mn you guys. Tell me the truth; I can take it. Didn't you see my face twitch? How about the time I tripped over the word 'progress?' That must have been cute! Wasn't I shouting?"

Of course the audience has to reassure him all over again that he made a fine presentation and how much he improved since that morning. I quietly rewind the tape and ask Joe to look at the monitor. When he sees a commanding presenter with strong eye contact delivering concise, coherent ideas in a powerful voice, his reaction is inevitably the same.

"Not bad," he'll say, "I sure don't look scared. Did I really do all that without notes?" His face is now just about glued to the screen and he pleasantly floats in his own quiet thoughts as I watch. He doesn't realize that I am now enjoying this moment as much as he.

I can be an annoying force when it comes to demanding my people be the best they can be in presentations. Sometimes I have to coax them; sometimes I bribe them;

sometimes, I even have to bully them (in a civilized way, of course); other times I'll act hurt if they won't try a technique or I might stand right next to them mimicking the movements I want them to do in front of the class until we're both laughing and the tension starts to dissipate.

No matter what I do, however, they seem to know I do it to get them to be their best. When they hear the reactions of their peers and see their images on the screen, they realize how good they can be and I only had their best interests at heart.

The monitor turns to electronic gray and the moment passes.

"Next?" I say. Another presenter frowns, pushes back his chair, and starts to walk towards the front of the room.

"Don't expect me to be as good as Joe!" he barks. "I hate presentations!"

I AM JOE'S AUDIENCE

(ORIGINALLY PUBLISHED IN *MEETINGS & CONVENTIONS*, 1981)

I still receive requests for "Joe's Audience" after more than a decade. A few presenters tell me they read it while they're involved in designing their 'anxiety strategy' or just before an important presentation. When I wrote the article, my purpose was to write a light, comfortable piece on presentations from the audience's perspective based on the Reader's Digest series of articles, "I Am Joe's Heart, Liver, etc." Although few of my seminar participants made the connection, they seemed to enjoy it just the same. I hope you will too.

I am Joe's audience.

I'm lots of different individuals but often I can be thought of as one thinking, feeling entity. Unfortunately, Joe doesn't think of me at all sometimes. Oh sure, he knows I exist, (if I didn't, there would be no reason for him to speak) but he doesn't think of his presentation in my terms. He only thinks of it in his own terms: his objectives, his needs, his fears. Although Joe is often with me listening to other presenters, when it's his turn to present, he forgets that he was ever a part of me. All of a sudden, I'm different. He assumes a whole new role and leaves me behind. And that's too bad. If Joe thought about a few simple things in my terms, his presentations would be much more effective

I want Joe to do well.

I may not want to buy everything Joe is trying to sell or accept each of his ideas, but I do want Joe to do well in his presentation. I don't want him to be extremely nervous or uncomfortable. That makes me uncomfortable. I don't want him to feel that I'm being overly critical about the way he talks or the way he looks. I'm not. Joe forgets that when he's part of an audience, he generally wants the speaker to do well. When he's the presenter, he often talks to himself in some pretty strange ways. He tells himself that he might make a fool of himself in front of me or it would be horrible if I didn't buy what he's trying to sell.

Naturally this negative self-talk results in anxiety. I wish he would just relax and do the best job he can. I'd certainly feel better about his presentations. And I know he would too.

I want Joe to treat me like a human being.

When I was a child, it was fun being read to. But now that I can read, it's annoying being read to. It's especially annoying when I know Joe knows what he'd like to tell me. He's just reading because he's afraid to talk to me like a person or worse, because he's unprepared. More than once, he's even read a "Good morning" to me! Now that's crazy!

Joe should treat me much as he treats other human beings. With respect. With understanding. With reason. He certainly should not be in awe of me or blame me for his feelings of nervousness. So often I've heard him say: "I really enjoy speaking to one person but I hate speaking to a group of people." There's no logic in that fear. If Joe can speak with authority and honesty to one individual human being, he can speak that way to a group of individual human beings. He's just got to speak louder, that's all.

I want to see Joe as a human being.

Sometimes when Joe puts on a business suit and starts speaking in technical terms with the seriousness of life and death, any resemblance he bears to an actual person is merely coincidental. I'd like to see Joe smile a bit and gesture with his hands in a natural way like he probably speaks to his friends and neighbors. And if he makes a mistake or two, or loses his train of thought for a moment, that's okay too. I want to see Joe as a person. I need to know and trust this person before I buy his product or ideas.

I can think faster than Joe can speak.

And I've got a lot to think about. That's why Joe must keep me interested with exciting words and vivid examples and situation to which I can immediately relate. I've been conditioned by years of television and instant everything.

Maybe my grandfather could sit back and think, and reflect, and concentrate, but I want good information fast. I really want Joe to tell me what he wants. I want him to lead the way (and at a good pace) logically from point to point.

I don't mean to sound harsh, but if Joe starts to ramble, I'll probably start to daydream or move ahead of him. I've done it for so many years that the expression on my face will never show that I'm not listening. Joe will look up and see me intently looking at him and think I'm listening, but I'll really be thinking of other things.

I need simplicity.

I can't stop Joe and put him on replay. If I miss a point or don't understand something, there's no stopping and going back as when I'm reading. And I probably won't bother to ask about it in the question-and-answer period either. So Joe must keep everything simple and repeat it often.

Often Joe tries to cram every point and every "important" piece of information into a short presentation. What he forgets is that nothing is important to me if I'm overwhelmed by it. And I'm always far more impressed with two or three simple key points supported by good documentation than I am with a mountain of facts, figures, statistics, expert testimony, the kitchen sink, and everything else he can think of to say. If Joe must communicate more information than I can handle in a short period of time, he can give it to me in a handout at the end of his presentation. If he's done his job well, I'll read it.

I want to know what I'm supposed to do.

Sometimes Joe speaks for an entire presentation and never clearly defines what it is he would like me to do. I know he wants me to do something or he probably wouldn't be speaking to me at all. And I guess it's probably something more than feel good about him or his company. I think Joe is afraid that if he asks me for a specific commitment, I'll say no. What he forgets is that if he doesn't ask, I can't say yes.

Joe has to be realistic in his request for an action (obviously I'm not going to spend hundreds of thousands of dollars of my company's money based on a 15-minute presentation) but he should get me to commit to something. Requesting me to do something can serve as an indication of the effectiveness of his talk.

I want Joe to finish.

Out of the thousands of times I've heard Joe give talks over the years, rarely have I ever been left with the feeling, "Gee, I wish he would speak longer." Most speakers speak far longer than they should and far longer than I'm willing to listen. I automatically tune out dull speakers or speakers that ramble. I also tune out good presenters who go on too long. My time is valuable. If a speaker requests 15 minutes of my time, that's about how much I'm willing to give.

I'm always impressed with presenters who cover exactly what they want to cover in the allotted time period and then end with an exciting conclusion. I know that speaker has taken the time to plan his presentation thoroughly and he respects me.

One last thing, Joe.

I want you to do well. I hope I'm not sounding like too much of an audience expert but the truth is: I am an audience expert. And so are you. And so is everyone else who ever sits in my place before you.

We know what we like. We know how we wish to be treated. And Joe, when you're in the audience, you know what you like and how you wish to be treated. If you would just put yourself in my seat when you plan your next presentation, it will be successful.

THE 10 MOST IMPORTANT THINGS TO REMEMBER ABOUT PRESENTATIONS

1. You don't have to be a great presenter to deliver a great presentation - but it's great to be a great presenter.

2. Above all else, when you present, you are presenting yourself.

3. If presentations were food, audiences would live on a diet of too much plain yogurt, non-fat cottage cheese, unflavored tofu, and skimmed milk. When it comes to your presentation, give 'em a little spumoni!

4. If you can't fix it fast, don't bring it! When the projector light bulb blows, the guy who does A-V is usually home watching T.V.

5. If a joke is relevant enough, clean enough, and funny enough to tell an audience, chances are they've heard it. If it isn't, they don't want to hear it anyway.

6. If you're hearing your presentation for the first time along with your audience, it probably doesn't sound too good to either of you.

7. IF IT DOESN'T ADD, IT SUBTRACTS.

8. It's not the audience's job to listen, it's the presenter's job to make them want to listen.

9. A presenter and an audience are like an egg and a rock. A presenter is responsible for every aspect of his presentation. It doesn't matter if the egg hits the rock or the rock hits the egg. In either case, it's not going to go well for the egg.

10. Nervous about your presentation? Think of the day, we hope many years from now, when you're lying on your deathbed listing the most significant events in your life. What number do you think this presentation is going to receive? - if you remember it at all.

A LETTER TO
CORPORATE AMERICA

If you're like most corporate presenters, Friend,

. . .we should talk. Think of your last presentation in business terms: how much did it cost for creation time, the fabrication and revision of countless visual aids, down time by employees or others as they listened to it, and your time? Now consider its effect: what changes occurred, what information was delivered, and what was even remembered in twenty-four hours by the majority of your audience?

Now let's think of it in human terms. Whom did you inspire? Whom did you motivate? Did you move information - or did you move people?

The average presentation in corporate America today is largely a waste of time that is neither efficient, cost-effective, nor successful in achieving its objectives. There's been a steady decrease in presentation effectiveness over the last few decades accompanied by a dramatic rise in cost. Company people expect to be bored during a large part of most presentations and they're seldom disappointed. Slick presentation "packages" are developed with costly pretty pictures for the wall and stirring, bulleted-point scripts, but they can't compensate for dull, uninspired presenters who aren't taught basic presentation skills.

Excellent visionary programs revolving around themes such as quality, strategic intent, and customer service often flounder because their true spirit and life can't be communicated through the ranks. What begins as an exciting new corporate direction crashes as some uninspired mope blandly plods through charts and graphs in an insipid attempt to explain the vision to an audience of those who must implement it. The results are predictable.

Why are we in this situation? There are undoubtedly many reasons but I have my own theory. I believe the great analytical minds which fueled the technology revolution in this country for the last forty years were perhaps not the best communicators to fellow human beings.

Please know I'm not being critical here; the chemical and electrical engineering brilliance of these people is what's chiefly responsible for America's predominance in many fields of technical endeavor. But as these extraordinary, scientifically oriented individuals rose through corporate ranks, they took with them an uncomfortableness regarding presentation communication that automatically condemned it to a position of low priority. While this may not have been critical as America enjoyed an unchallenged position of technical superiority, it became a significant liability as corporations grew, became more complex, and faced increased competition.

To make matters worse, the culture also began to change and younger employees raised on television came to expect short bursts of crystallized information accompanied by exciting graphics. Of course this created even more pressure on senior management which was not even prepared to meet the presentation standards of a less demanding time.

Jumping into the communication abyss came a plethora of fast vendors hawking expensive, flashing, whirring bandaids designed to present for presenters - rather than help them present. Once again, the results are predictable and that's pretty much the situation today.

Is the situation hopeless?

Not by any means! I refuse to believe that the same brilliant minds who delivered the magic technology that is allowing my thoughts to be instantly word processed through my fingers at this moment cannot recognize the problem and devise a strategy to solve it.

The solution is easy - it's getting to that solution that needs some work. The answer is getting back to the basics of efficient human communication which includes clear objectives, simple points, and a standardized structure so people can easily understand our message. How do we get there? That will be different for every corporate culture that exists. But I know the journey is vital and the rewards will be great.

One person who believes you have the wisdom and the courage to begin is . . .

yours truly,

Frank Paolo

JUMP!
(My "closing" to this book.)

Two years ago, I stood before the worst presentation seminar class I've ever experienced. Two out of the six people were openly antagonistic and a third was loud and rude. The other three people seemed intimidated by the villains and were of little help until the end of the seminar when they turned in anonymous, exemplary evaluations, complimenting my professionalism, patience, and fortitude.

What was puzzling about this group was the fact that their counterparts, whom I had coached previously, were ideal students who were willing to question their erroneous beliefs about presentations and try do something about them with my coaching. Their efforts were rewarded. They began to give superior speeches and their manager later told me so in a letter.

So I stupidly assumed the second group would do about the same. This is the equivalent of arriving at a critical presentation and walking up to an untested microphone with nothing to say and starting with a joke you hope you can remember. In other words, a disaster waiting to happen. It hit about three minutes into the day, when I was just beginning to lay the groundwork for the very first module.

"This is the same old crap we learned as MBA's," piped up one antagonist, "it just doesn't work in the real world."

Let me tell you something about good professional speakers. By the time you hear someone in public who's actually getting paid a decent fee to speak, you can be sure that person has been around the block a few times. If he's had fifteen or twenty years of speaking experience, you can also bet he's run into his share of hecklers, drunks, jerks, psychotics, malcontents, dweeps, nitwits, and dolts.

The outbursts from these types are usually more amusing than threatening to a good speaker because most audience members are already on our side, we have many retorts to squelch annoying eruptions, and hecklers give us great opportunities to demonstrate these "spontaneous" comebacks. (Oops, there goes another secret.) Often the only choice a professional presenter faces is choosing which retort will be effective and will not adversely affect other audience members. Inexperienced presenters err on the side of sledgehammers, good presenters favor needles.

When the idiot interrupted, I could have delivered any number of well-rehearsed replies. I could have said, for example, "I'm sorry, are you speaking now for the entire class or just yourself?" (This is really a no-win question for the rude one. He knows he can't speak for everyone but he is using up everyone's time.) I'd continue, "If you're speaking just for yourself perhaps your manager and I could work something out so you could make better use of your time today." (This, obviously, would be rather difficult for him to explain to his manager since that gentleman was the one who demanded he take my seminar in the first place.)

Or I could have said, "You mean you know this material and already do it well?   Great!   The only problem is I'm being paid to teach it to you but I'll tell you what I'll do. I'll give you a few minutes to prepare a short presentation that we can video and show your management. If you do it well, I'll not only have my office refund what you paid for the course, I'll double it out of my own pocket."

In the half dozen or so times I've been forced to use this line over the years, I've never had to give a refund. Actually, no one has even accepted the challenge.

But since it was only three minutes into the seminar and I wasn't convinced the dweeb's anger wasn't really fear mixed with bravado (a common reaction from many macho poor presenters), I let it slide with a little "buddy" approach.

"Look friend," I smiled, "that's a pretty heavy charge to be leveling at my whole seminar when you've only heard the first few minutes. Why don't you give me a chance to present some ideas to you and then make a decision about it?" When he laughed, I immediately knew I had made a mistake. While most of the world's creatures respond well to civilized behavior, bullies interpret consideration as weakness.

The lout was on me again in minutes and then his toad-brained friend jumped into the fray. To make matters worse, both were terrible presenters and refused to try anything new. It took every ounce of professionalism I could muster not to ridicule them as they stood in front of the class defending the triteness and banality that had characterized their dull dumps of mindless, disorganized drivel.

By the mid-morning break I had used the line reserved only for the most hopeless of sessions (utilized just two or three times previously in my life), "I get paid either way. You can become better presenters with my help or not. It doesn't matter in the least to me." By lunch we were openly insulting to each other.

As the afternoon dragged to a close, one of the imbeciles said, "I know we gave you a hard time today but why didn't you teach us what you taught the other group? Did you give them the good stuff so we'd look bad?"

As you may have noticed, this is a long story and it really doesn't make me look very good. I'm risking that to make a very important point to you. Both groups were given exactly the same information in pretty much the same way with any difference favoring the clods because of my eagerness to meet their challenge in a professional manner. The real difference between the two groups can be summarized in one word: attitude. And that's why what you're about to read may well be more important than anything you've read in this book.

The words you are now reading can help you make one great presentation, help you become a great presenter, or be dismissed completely. The only difference is in your attitude - how you wish to relate to these words. The ideas in this book are the same for every reader. There will be some readers who haven't even read this far (there they are now, watching reruns of "Cheers"); others will pick up the book, make a simple great presentation and save the book for their next presentation opportunity. That's fine, - they got good value for their time and money. I hope they enjoyed the ride.

And this is where most people get off the bus.

For the next few pages, I'd like to speak with the remaining passengers, those people whom I've inspired to go beyond the confines of a simple formula; those who may decide to take the time and trouble to become great presenters.

Got your tickets, friends?

I know much of the material in this book may have been new or different from things you thought you knew about presentations. That's as it should be. But you should also know that new or different ideas are the easiest to ridicule and dismiss because they're not familiar, comfortable, tested and found 100 percent safe by the FDA and every living soul.

You know, for example, exactly what audiences will do when they hear a "good morning" opening. Nothing. They expect to hear that opening and will be surprised to hear anything else. Breaking new ground always involves risks.

What are the risks in delivering an exciting opening or any other new or different effective presentation technique? Figure it out yourself. It's always risky to be different. But some of my presenters want a guarantee. "Are you sure it's O.K. to cut this many details, structure it like this, deemphasize visual aids, ad nauseum. Are you 100 percent sure?"

No - I'm not sure. I'm about 90 percent sure but I refuse to baby grownups. You must make your own assessment - you must take the risk. After all, you will reap the rewards. Do you want them for nothing? Uh-uh. If rewards were given for nothing, everyone would have them and they'd be worth what everyone paid (and the bus would be damned crowded at this point).

In presentations, you have one huge factor that tips the

risk/reward ratio in your favor: the status quo. If you've read just about any other section of this book, you know what I think.

Most presenters bore most audience members most of the time in most presentations.

So what wonderful thing exactly are you risking by continuing to do what you do? Your ability to blend into the dull gray? The bleak option of being instantly forgettable and forgotten? The dreary choice of having an audience ignore you and your ideas?

Assuming you are a person who has the backbone and guts to take reasonable risks for greater rewards, can you see the tremendous potential for yourself in communicating more effectively?

Can you imagine the magic involved in moving people, not information? Can you fantasize what it would be like to mesmerize an entire roomful of individual human beings if only for a few seconds and change the way they look at the world? Can you imagine the power, the excitement, the experience?

You know I think you can do it. You have the material right here to begin. The only real question is, do you think you can do it?

"Sure," you might think, "easy for him to say. He probably always was good in presentations and just refined a fluke talent."

You're absolutely right, of course. I was very fortunate to have a natural talent for communication, the best parents in the world, some great professors along the way, and some clients who trusted me enough to allow me to fail grandly a few times.

No one could ask for more But I'm not this fortunate in everything and my last story may show you why I feel I have the audacity to speak to the parts of you which still might be apprehensive about taking the risks to become a great presenter. I do so with the utmost consideration and respect.

I've always been afraid to fly. I don't know how they stay up there and I don't care. So if it's more dangerous to ride in an automobile, how come I've survived three serious car wrecks (two totals) with nary a scratch and they count the few "survivors" as lucky if they live through a plane crash? (If they were really lucky, they would have taken the train by mistake.)

So when I was young and brave, I decided to tweak my fear in a lofty way to prove to myself that irrational fear would never rule my life. For my twenty-fifth birthday, I decided to parachute out of a plane. My friends were shocked and supportive in their usual way:

"How can you jump out of the plane, if you're too scared to take off in it?"

"We'll show up with sponges and blotters just in case this turns out to be a bad idea."

"Don't worry about the chute opening, you'll be dead of shock long before that!"

After a day of jump training, minutes before boarding the small Cessna on that warm spring afternoon, I approached the director of the school, a seasoned jumper from Italy who was making his living in America. He seemed to me a wonderful blend of old world good sense and new world adventure.

"Franco," I said, "what happens if a jumper gets to the open door, looks down 3000 feet and just decides it isn't worth it? What do you say to him then?"

Franco looked at me with kind, understanding eyes. It was a look that cut through different cultures, and macho, and bullshit. He turned up to the sky watching another jumper.

"I don't say nothing, of course. No one does. Hey, what can we say? You make the choice. You can jump - take the short way down - and experience the most thrilling thing in your life or you can relax and land with the pilot. Nobody's going to say nothing."

I thought of those words as I jumped into nothing and felt the hard snap of the chute as it was yanked open by the static line. In a split second, I luxuriated in the most breathtaking ride of my life for about two or three minutes. I felt things I had never felt before and experienced things I've never experienced since.

For a brief moment, I was a part of the sky. My life would never be the same again.

Friend, your parachute is packed inside this book. Your plane will be in the air the next time you stand before an audience and the door will be open. That's the moment you'll have to decide between jumping into the sky of exciting presentations or relaxing and landing with only that which is expected of you.

If I'm in your audience and you choose to land with the pilot, I won't say anything. I won't criticize or belittle you. Promise. In fact, I'll probably be blaming myself for not having the talent nor the technique to inspire you.

But if you jump, you'll recognize me sooner. I'll be the one jumping to my feet at the end of your presentation, clapping and grinning and yelling like a madman. I'll be the first one to recognize your gamble and your triumph in effective human communication. Please pay my embarrassing exuberance no attention.

Your success will be my reward.

A QUICK REFERENCE GUIDE TO 175 PRESENTATION IDEAS IN THIS BOOK

Your Audience

		Page
1	Choose one audience member	19
2	Choose most important member	19
3	Choose representative member	20
4	See your audience as bell curve	20
5	Do a good audience analysis	21
6	Seat audience "in front of you"	22
7	Bridge audience knowledge gap	23
8	Do separate talks if necessary	23
9	Consider some pre-talk reading	24
10	Consider post-talk reading	24
11	Aim talk high if necessary	25
12	Learn what audience likes	25
13	Decide: concepts or details?	26
14	Shape his view of you	27
15	Shape his view of you more	28
16	Dress to present	28
17	Present a positive attitude	30
18	Present some enthusiasm!	31
19	Pretend you're enthused	32
20	Write your introduction	34
21	Audience step - Summary	36

Your Objective

22   Form the objective 40
23   If it doesn't add, it subtracts 40
24   Eliminate all tangents 41
25   Stick to objective always! 41
26   Stick to one objective always 43
27   State objective every time? 44
28   Every objective every time? 44
29   Agree with audience always 45
30   Write objective and send it 45
31   Never disagree with audience 46
32   Write your objective first 46
33   How critical is objective? 47
34   Objective as a poker hand 47
35   Objective step - Summary 48

Your Support Structure

36   Don't present without structure 49
37   Limit your points severely........................50
38   Limit them more! Simplify 51
39   Understanding learning factors 52
40   Always number your points! 52
41   Use other structures rarely 53
42   Simplify! Simplify! Simplify!....................53
43   Simplicity vs. superficiality 54
44   Limit points to two or three words 54
45   Help yourself with structure 55
46   Use simplicity with high ethics 56
47   Structure step - Summary........................57
48   Examples of Objectives and their
      Supporting Points 58

Your Visual Aids

49 Change your mind on visuals! 63
50 Consider what can go wrong 65
51 Don't talk about your visuals...................65
52 What to do if visuals required...................66
53 Create active visual aids 69
54 Example of active visual aid...................69
55 Use room light open/close 66
56 Learn more about visuals...................67
57 Write off "write alongs" 68
58 Decide visual screen time 68
59 Use visuals as questions 69
60 Don't talk about visuals 69
61 Don't apologize for visuals...................69
62 Visualize Gettysburg address...................70
63 Visual aid step - Summary 70
64 Use microphones correctly...................70

Explain Your Points

65 Try very hard to simplify 75
66 Make your presentation simpler...................77
67 See what 'more details' means 78
68 Don't judge only by audience...................78
69 Don't give information dumps...................78
70 Give audience too few details 79
71 Try to learn to like simplicity...................80
72 Reconsider "technical" details 80
73 Don't let the "expert" speak...................81
74 State your conclusions first 82
75 Consider details vs. analysis 83
76 Deliver details differently...................83
77 Explain step - Summary...................83

Your Opening

78   Relieve anxiety with opening 85
79   Involve audience immediately...............................87
80   Distinguish yourself from others 88
81   Forget Memorization 89
82   Don't use jokes as openers 90
83   Separate jokes and humor......................................91
84   Deliver a dramatic statement................................91
85   Ask a rhetorical question 92
86   "Get 'em noddin' "...93
87   "Approval from back row" 93
88   Beware of real questions 93
89   Turn real question into negative 94
90   Raise your hand 94
91   Deliver a personal experience.............................95
92   Obey three rules for experience 96
93   Open with a slice-of-life 97
94   Only use the proper prop......................................98
95   No quotes for openers 100
96   No definitions either 100
97   Opening step - Summary.......................................100

Your Conclusion

98   Don't thank audience 103
99   Think of an economic exchange 104
100 Don't be a boot-licking pleaser 104
101 Beware audience reaction......................................105
102 Use same opening methods...................................107
103 Use an open/close match 107
104 Beat by "best" match...108
105 Put yourself in their seat close 109
106 Deliver one more thing close 110
107 Ask for order close 110

108 Use pauses effectively 111
109 Conclusion step - Summary 113

Your Preview, et al.

110 Tell 'em what you're gonna 114
111 Preview et al. explained 115
112 Use to help with transitions 117
113 Create open/close after.............................117
114 Use this to help create open...................118

Your Anxiety

115 You must end your anxiety......................119
116 Experience presentation pleasure 120
117 Pay the cost of anxiety 120
118 Understanding your anxiety 123
119 Understanding Ellis theory.......................123
120 Avoid irrational sentences........................125
121 Don't become a symptom expert 126
122 Cure irrational fear 127
123 Understand reality sentences 128
124 Copy these sentences on a card.............129
125 Develop process for sentences 129
126 Understand the process.............................130
127 Believe the results 132
128 Don't get derailed by boredom 129
129 Review the process 133
130 Don't relax completely..............................133
131 Learn your physical response 134
132 Learn why thinking ceases........................135
133 Learn to manually override 136
134 Learn to relax shoulders 136
135 Learn to breath deeply..............................137

136 Learn when to use these................................137
137 Utilize good sense 137
138 Learn audience reaction 138
139 Anxiety-Reducing Strategy 139
140 Note 'too much' warning 141

Your Rehearsal

141 Learn importance of rehearsal 144
142 Learn three levels of rehearsal 145
143 Spend the time it takes.............................145
144 Forget a quick fix 146
145 Speak twice as loud...................................147
146 Learn real reasons for loudness 148
147 Beat womens' disadvantage 150
148 Overcome another one!...............................151
149 Use tape & video recorders 151
150 Change your words-it's ok 152
151 Determine how loud to speak 152
152 Forget overrehearsing.................................153
153 You can't rehearse silently........................153
154 Rehearsal step - Summary.........................154

Your Audience's Judgment

155 Control prepresentation image.....................157
156 Master audience contact.............................158
157 Increase your enthusiasm 159
158 Assume your authority 159
159 Deliver a great presentation 160

Don't Take Dumb Advice

160 Don't generalize! 162
161 Don't rehearse in mirror! 163
162 Don't imagine them naked! 164
163 Don't wing it! 164
164 Don't have a few belts! 166
165 Don't read a script! 167
166 Don't be informal! 168
167 Don't pace back & forth! 169
168 Don't use quotations! 170
169 Don't squeeze your digits! 173
170 Don't borrow this book! 174

Don't Make Excuses

171 Learn from other peoples' 175

Read An Old Article

172 Read "I Am Joe's Audience" 178

Read a Good List

173 Read '10 Important Things'......................183

Read Author's Closing

174 Read "Jump!" 188
175 Call Frank Paolo! 202

ABOUT THE AUTHOR

Frank Paolo is a consultant for corporate presentations. He resides in Rochester, New York with his wife Tracy and their cats, Sunday and Monday. He is available for lectures, seminars, and consultation, and provides a money-back guarantee on their success (virtually unique in the world of professional speaking). For more information on fees and available dates, please contact:

Mr. Frank Paolo
Frank Paolo, Inc,
Box 4-V
10 Manhattan Square
Rochester, New York 14607
(716) 546-3244

INDEX

Anxiety - 119-141
Anxiety, strategy to stop - 139
Anxiety, understanding your -122-125
Approval from back - 93
Ask for the order - 110
Audience - 19-37
Audience analysis - 25, 26
Audience bell curve - 20
Audience contact - 22
Audience knowledge gap - 23-25
Audience likes - 25
Audience members - 19-23
Audience members naked - 164
Audience's view - 21-22
Authority - 56, 57

Boredom - 192, 88
Breathing - ???
Bush, George W. - 120

Conclusions - 103-113
Conclusions stated first - 82
Conclusions, one more thing - 110

Definitions as openers - 100
Detail alternatives - 83
Detail or concept oriented? - 26
Details - 78-82
Details, few - 79
Details, what's enough? - 78
Dramatic statement - 91-92
Dress, presentation - 28-30
Dumb advice, - 162
Dump, information - 78

Ellis, Dr. Albert - 122-133
Enthusiasm! - 30-31
Ethics, presentation - 57
Excuses - 175-177
Experts - 81-82

Generalization - 162-163
Gettysburg address - 70
Greetings - 100

Hands, raise - 94-95

Introduction - 33-36

Joe's Audience - 178-182
Jokes vs. Humor - 90-91
Jump! - 188-194

Learning factors - 52
Loudness - 72-74, 147-151

Memorization - 89-90
Microphones - 70-74
Mirrors - 163-164

Noddin' - 93

Objective - 39-48
Objective first - 46-47
Objective stated? - 44
Objective, importance - 39, 47
Objective, written - 45
Objectives, examples - 58-60
Open/close match - 107-109
Opening jokes - 90-91
Openings - 85-101
Openings as relief - 89
Openings, audience involvement - 87-88
Openings, distinguishing - 88-89
Openings, personal experience - 95-97
Openings, slice-of-life - 97
Over-rehearsing - 153

Pacing - 169
Pauses - 111-112

Pleasers - 104-106
Points, explain - 75-83
Points, limited - 50
Points, numbered - 52
Post-talk reading - 24
Pre-talk reading - 24
Preview·go-through·review - 114-116
Props - 98-99

Questions, real - 93-94
Quotes - 170-173

Reality sentences - 128-133
Rehearsal - 143-154
Rehearsal, silent - 153
Relaxation, physical - 136-137
Rhetorical questions - 92-93
Rockefeller, Nelson A. - 120
Room light open/close - 66-67

Separate presentations - 23-24
Simplicity - 77-82
Simplify! - 53-54
Step 1 - 3, 29-37
Step 2 - 3, 39-48
Step 3 - 4, 49-60
Step 4 - 6, 63-74
Step 5 - 8, 75-83
Step 6 - 10, 85-101
Step 7 - 12, 103-118
Step 8 - 12, 119-141
Step 9 - 14, 143-154
Structure - 55
Structure, limited points - 54-55
Summary of Steps - 15
Sunday & Monday - 41-42
Supporting points - 50, 58-60

Tangents - 41
Thank you's - 103-104

Visual aids - 63-74
Visuals as questions - 69
Visuals, "active" - 6
Visuals, don't talk about - 65-66, 69

Winging It - 164-166
Write-along visuals - 68
Worrying - 119-141